Hello Soul!

Endorsements

"Alena opened her soul and responded with this magnificent book. She was guided to open her heart and receive the goodness around her, and I suggest you do the same by following the brilliant guidance in *Hello Soul*."

Peggy McColl, *New York Times* best-selling author

ALENA CHAPMAN

hello
Soul

EVERYDAY WAYS
TO BEGIN AWAKENING
YOUR SPIRITUALITY

NEW YORK

LONDON • NASHVILLE • MELBOURNE • VANCOUVER

hello, soul!

Everyday Ways to Begin Awakening Your Spirituality
and Live by Your Soul

Published in New York, New York, by Morgan James Publishing. Morgan James is a trademark of Morgan James, LLC. www.MorganJamesPublishing.com

Proudly distributed by Publishers Group West®

A **FREE** ebook edition is available for you
or a friend with the purchase of this print book.

_____

CLEARLY SIGN YOUR NAME ABOVE

Instructions to claim your free ebook edition:
1. Visit MorganJamesBOGO.com
2. Sign your name CLEARLY in the space above
3. Complete the form and submit a photo
   of this entire page
4. You or your friend can download the ebook
   to your preferred device

ISBN 9781631955082 paperback
ISBN 9781631955099 ebook
Library of Congress Control Number:
2021930906

Cover and Interior Design by:
Chris Treccani
www.3dogcreative.net

Morgan James is a proud partner of Habitat for Humanity Peninsula
and Greater Williamsburg. Partners in building since 2006.

Get involved today! Visit: www.morgan-james-publishing.com/giving-back

Dedication

This book is dedicated to those who feel unfulfilled and know there must be more to living this life! It is your time to shine!

Contents

Acknowledgments

Grateful acknowledgement I have immense gratitude for all the incredible mentors, friends, and people who believed in the journey and helped me in my growth! Special gratitude to my amazing friend Erin Saxton for her belief in me and the mission of guiding others to happier and fulfilling lives and this book and to Chad Lefevre for his continued honesty and wanting to make this mission a reality for all. Many thanks to Peter Hoppenfeld for his encouragement and patience while I wrote *Hello Soul*. I am grateful to my editor, Stephanie Gunning, for her understanding, striving for my betterment as an author, and her guidance. I feel tremendous appreciation for my sons, Stevie, James, and Danny, for their continued support and love. Thank you also to Elizabeth Gilbert—without our interview I would have never found my true mission to serve others in their spiritual growth. Heartfelt thanks as well to all the friends who have read the book and experienced living by their souls.

Author's Note

Every religion and mode of belief has a different concept of, and name for God or the One. For me, the word *God* has too many meanings that simply do not correspond with my own conceptual ideal of the ultimate, unconditionally loving, powerful, everything-and-nothing, beautiful Source. Because of all the blessings I have received, I call this incredible presence the Beloved and sometimes my Divine Beloved. And the vast and all-knowing Universe is, to me, the Divine Universe. You may always use whatever words reach deep inside you that you feel open you to the Ultimate Being of your personal belief system and swap those in for mine when you read them.

For most of my life, I have been both religious and spiritual, perhaps because of my past career in the field of music. I have conducted choirs in churches and temples associated with many different religions beginning at age eighteen. Because of my spiritual nature, I found the Beloved in absolute splendor in every song and loving scripture of every religion I was privileged to serve. Our spiritual side is what brings the Beloved into the religion of our hearts.

Unfortunately, I was an unconscious competent in my spirituality. I thought everyone felt the same incredible feeling of love and acceptance that I did. When I took a turn in my life where I left my career in music, my spirituality, and my natural connection to my soul behind me, I found my life changed to a mundane existence filled with heavy darkness, pettiness, constant busyness, and emptiness.

I had to find my way back to the magic of the Beloved. But first I had to hear my true essence, my soul. I had to accept its beauty inside myself before connecting to the Beloved, the world, and the Divine Universe. Thus, my journey began.

My journey was filled with discovery, interest and fun. I never felt that any part of this journey was hard. I was surprised by all the amazing teachers and experiences brought into my path to learn and grow.

That is why I invite you, the reader, to join me. Everything I learned and how I learned it is in this book. Use it, adapt it, and make it a part of your own journey! You deserve, as much as I did, to live a life in full connection with your soul. You deserve to say "Hello, Soul" and hear a hello back.

Introduction

"Hello Soul! How may I serve today?"
"Alena, just open your heart and receive
the goodness all around you."

Another glorious morning! "Good morning, Universe/ God. How may I serve today? What is in store?" I ask, as I stretch my waking body to the new day.

During the day, I feel happy and excited about the journey I am on. Are there challenges? Yes, of course. As I, my family, and my business grow, there are challenges—bumps in the road. But these bumps stimulate our growth. However, there is more ease and flow as I move through the obstacles. I am not alone, because I open myself to the guidance of spirit. Whenever I want guidance, I ask my soul and the answers come to me either as thoughts or in the form of experiences and opportunities. I feel complete and happy!

Does this sound farfetched or strange? Is it *really* possible to live this way?

When we are children, we are much more likely to live from our souls. We understand why we are here. Our talents are flowing freely from us in every way we play, interact, and accomplish our growing tasks. Our imaginations are wide open. Anything is possible.

It is when we are taught what it is right to think and be that we become detached from our true essence, our deepest self, our soul. We conform to a world that society has created. Our soul lies waiting deep inside of us. Waiting for us to wake up from this conformity sleep.

What is the soul really? It is a cloud of energy—and there are many levels to it. Part of it animates our bodies. Part of it is perpetually connected to the Beloved—to God/the Universe. It is around us and in us, and it is the essence of us that knows why we were born and why we have come to live this life on earth. When I speak of the soul, I sometimes say I am *with* it or *in* it (or it is *in* me), but I also sometimes say I am living *from* it—meaning I am aligned with this essence and adhering to its guidance.

I have been blessed in so many ways. I live wide awake with my soul. For a significant part of my life, I have lived my purpose. Through music, nature, and a sense of freedom, I felt my craving for the amazing presence of the Beloved in my life. I really cannot express how miraculous I felt the world was. Everything I did turned into beauty and gold. The more divine presence I felt, the more gifts came into my life. Most of all, I was feeling joy and I had the powerful, inner knowing that I was fine and would always be fine no matter what.

Then, at the age of thirty-eight, I began to listen to people I respect tell me how to live. Following the expectations of others, conforming to what is "normal," I began to lose my connection to the presence of the Beloved and my soul. Consciously, I knew the Universe was there. I just didn't feel it. Along with my loss of connection to this amazing presence, I lost a big part of me: my dreams, my love for living, seeing the miraculous, and a feeling of immense, never-ending possibility and accomplishment.

Life lost its magic! It felt heavy and difficult to endure. Every day felt as if it had the same challenges, expectations, and events in it. People were judgmental, and sometimes harsh. There was no adventure or discovery. It seemed that everyone around me wanted sameness, or more precisely, safety. I was bored and becoming very sarcastic. But really, I was feeling lost without the constant high of feeling connected to the deepest part of myself. Where did she go? *Are heaviness and hardship normal?* I would wonder.

"This is life," people told me. "You have everything anyone could ever want. Your social standing comes with expectations, with things you must do. Most important are the needs of your husband and family—what you do now is for them," I was told while holding my newborn first child in my arms. Of course, my children and family were important to me, but did that mean I had to sacrifice all of myself for them, and everything I had worked so hard for since I was fifteen years old? Was I supposed to only live through them and their achievements? How would I be happy if I was only a shadow of myself?

I kept trying to make my marriage work—to be the so-called perfect wife, do what was expected from me, and live the way my husband wanted to live. At the same time, inside, I heard a voice asking me questions. *Must life be this way—so heavy, so hard? Are we supposed to expect so little of ourselves and our lives? Must we live "safely" within the confines of rules and expectations? Do we have to lose ourselves—shelve our dreams, hopes, and voices—to please those around us?*

The voice became louder and louder until I couldn't ignore it anymore! Finally, I knew it was time to rediscover the vivacious woman in me who loves life and herself. I longed for the magic to come back! It was time to open my heart and sing loudly, to say: "Hello, dear Soul! I am coming home."

It is funny how fast the Beloved/Divine Universe acts when you firmly decide to do something. The very next day, information flowed into me on how to begin. I understood not to be afraid, not to judge, but instead to discover, feel, give, forgive, and truly let go. Slowly, I felt the beautiful soul of Alena reemerge. I became happy again—genuinely happy deep down. Each morning after that, I woke with a small sensation of excitement for what the day held for me. What would I discover next?

My gratitude and love of nature led me to take gardening classes, and soon I became a master gardener. I found I had a talent for designing landscapes—the mixing of colors and textures of plants was fun—and people began hiring me to design their gardens. My soul began to sing. I found more flow and joy in every moment. I was coming home!

However, the more I lived by my true essence, the less pleased my husband became. He did not welcome the emergence of my soul. Nor did his family welcome it. I no longer fit into their box. According to them, I was not supposed to work in other people's gardens. I was not supposed to work at all. My decision to keep operating my small, creative, fun business despite my husband's objections and my in-laws sniping at me caused our marriage to spiral quickly into divorce.

Sure, I could have chosen simply to work on my own gardens at home, which looked magnificent. But bringing creativity and beauty into other people's lives gave me a strong sense of accomplishment and gratitude and wonder. Even more importantly, I had begun to believe in magic again, and I didn't want to give that up. Each day felt like a miracle. It was as if I was opening more and more of my heart to my soul with every landscape I designed and installed.

I could not understand why my husband didn't enjoy having a happy, creative person in his life—or at the very least, allow me to be me. Instead, he became very unhappy. Maybe he found it hard to watch someone else finding her joy and living each day as a gift when he felt stuck and limited. Whatever the reason, it was clear our marriage couldn't survive.

I will not say that my journey back to living with my soul and in the awesome presence of the Beloved has been easy. I can say, however, that every challenge my family and I go through, including the ones that led to my divorce, is spurring me to become who I always knew deep inside—a spiritual thought leader and mystic. The more I grew on my own journey back to the magic showed me why I can help so many other people say hello to their souls and to have the peace, and deep contentment in their lives.

Amid the difficult circumstances of my divorce, the Beloved/Divine Universe brought in *tools:* clarifying activities and concepts that enabled me to live more in my soul and help my growing children. Indeed, these were miraculous tools. The more I used these skills for living and applied what I was learning, the more support I was able to offer. We were able to transcend the difficulty of our household's transition instead of getting swallowed up in our feelings about it. My life lessons became easier to learn, and the kids and I grew stronger as a family.

Of course, there were times I felt upset, confused, and even scared. There were times when my faith would falter, and I could not hear my soul. It was a learning experience. Each time the struggle of my divorce brought me down, I found that with the tools I could connect faster. There were even times the Divine Universe would step in and help. I recovered from my upset faster and felt more in control. As long as I stayed disciplined and used the tools, my heart remained open and my vision clear. Honestly, I was amazed at how fast I was growing spiritually despite circumstances that were far from ideal.

It would be so easy for you to read my story and say, "That's fine for you, Alena. But you don't know what I am living through." And you're right. I do not know what your life is like or the struggles you face. However, I do know that now, more than ever, is the time to begin to open up and listen to that small voice inside you.

We all know what is in our hearts. We have a feeling that things can be different. If you open to that inner voice—the one who knows you are capable of true happiness, achievement, and love, and how to get those things—you will find you finally have the courage to change your circumstances. You will not feel alone anymore. And all it takes is learning how to open to your divine self!

Join me in *Hello, Soul!* as I share with you the story of how I opened myself to my soul and the experiences, lessons, and people the Divine Universe brought to me. This journey of lessons provides the "how" I needed to realize my dreams and lead a life of fulfillment and joy—and this "how" will work for you as well. For now, it is your turn. All you need to do is open your soul to enjoy reading about the journey and discipline yourself to practice and learn from my experience. There are tools and exercises included at the back of each chapter that are designed to guide your heart to experience the magic of your soul.

Don't we owe it to ourselves and those close to us to try—and better yet, achieve—a life worth living? Isn't it time to honestly believe and trust that you are here on earth for a reason and your Beloved/Divine Universe is walking with you? Isn't it worth saying, "Hello, my dear soul, . . . are you there?"

So, join me and begin to open yourself to that special place inside—your soul. To hear its gentle, but strong voice of pure love speaking to you and draw upon its strength.

In fact, you can try it right now. Close your eyes and breathe deeply. See yourself as strong, happy, and having inner peace. Begin to remember that girl or boy you once were who was true to who she or he was—free, brave, fun, enjoying the present, hopeful, and excited for the future.

Got an image? How does it feel to remember who you were back then?

When we were children, we lived more in our souls—our essences. We felt free to try anything. Nothing seemed a challenge or an impossibility. Instead, everything was seen as something new and exciting. If someone didn't like us—oh well, there were others to play with during recess. I used to swing very high, trying to touch my toes to the sky. And why not?

Do we need to be children again in order to hear our souls? No. However, when you do discover the essence inside—your soul—you can expect again to feel like that young girl or boy you once were. The world will open to you the same way it did when you were young and totally connected to your soul.

In this book, I am on a journey. I invite you to join me and to say these words: "Hello, Soul! It has been such a long time. I am so excited to come home to you!"

Take a leap of faith with me. What do you have to lose? Come with me through all my experiences and discovery and learn the same tools and concepts that I learned from friends, teachers, and sometimes the Divine Universe itself. We will have fun and, at the very least grow in our own awareness. As you read these pages, I encourage you to become engrossed in the journey. Learn and practice the skills associated with each lesson and, in the process, you will come to feel more open and at peace.

The beauty of connecting with your soul is that it starts with making a simple choice, and then just doing it! Your soul is waiting for you! It has been quiet for a long time, but it is ready to greet the world again.

It is time to rise above the messiness of your daily life and gain profound clarity about matters that seem murky to you. You are ready for the truth—I know this because why else would you have bought a book called *Hello, Soul?* You are ready to fulfill the reason you came to Earth—to fulfill your purpose and dreams.

Let's not waste any more time. Please give yourself permission to take the life-changing journey of reconnecting with your soul—of discovering the true you. You, my dear, deserve this, just as I did. Everything you need is here when you are ready to commit to accepting what truly is your birthright. It is time to be your magnificent, beautiful, miraculous true self.

Chapter 1

Mundane to Magic

Life is a journey that can be magical or mundane.
We are the ones to choose.

For most of my life, I have been an unconscious competent. An *unconscious competent* is someone who unconsciously attains whatever she wants without understanding how it is happening. My mother always used to say that I must have a rabbit's foot hidden in my pocket. As a child, I lived in the magic of synchronicities—unbelievable opportunities filled my life. It felt like the Universe had opened my mind. And it all began at the early age of seven years.

It was on a day when I decided to pretend to be sick so that I could stay home. As I sat in my bed looking out my windows at the big flakes of snow falling gently over the landscape, I caught a movement out of the side of my eye. I looked over to the pictures of two little girl ballerinas with big heads on my wall. These were my favorite pictures because I loved to dance and wanted to be a ballerina. As I looked at the ballerinas now, their lips moved, and I heard them speak in my head. These pretty and graceful girls were talking to me.

Later in life, I always wondered why I didn't scream or run. I simply was not afraid. I sensed that they were not evil or trying to harm me. I was curious and amazed. The ballerinas said I had a gift, and never to be afraid of it, because my gift came from God. My gift was to help souls walk into the light.

The way this was explained to me was that when a soul misses going to the light/heaven the first time then I can help it understand that it wouldn't be judged, and it was simply going home.

The first thing I did after receiving this information was to jump out of bed and run down to my mother. The gift was so special! I was so excited to have it that I wanted to share the news with everyone.

"Mom, my ballerinas can talk . . . and they told me that I was to help everyone go to the light—me, Mom! Their lips moved! I do so want to be a pretty ballerina." In my excitement, words poured incoherently from my mouth as I waved my arms in the air.

Once my mother calmed me down and understood what I was saying, her face turned white and her mouth formed a firm, straight line.

"This is not a gift," she said. "You are not to share this with anyone! Our house must be haunted. You have been tricked!" Despite her words, I felt a comforting presence surrounding me. It was pure love, confirming that my gift was true and came from God. I listened and thought, *I will never tell anyone else about my gift as long as I live because they won't be able to understand.*

The Beloved and Divine Universe really gave me a second gift on that snowy day. The first was my gift to help the fearful spirits of people go into the light after they died. The second was a feeling of love that was pure and open. I had never felt anything like it. Yes, my mom and dad did love me and would do everything they could for me. I felt their love all the time. But the love I felt from the Divine Universe was different.

Maybe that is why from that day forth I have felt different. I found that I did not worry, like everyone else seemed to, about school or friends. I was always popular although I never felt like I belonged exclusively to any group.

I attended a religious school. What my parents and teachers found interesting was how I seemed so full of love for God without being influenced by the dogmas of Catholicism.

As I grew up, everything simply fell into place for me. I was never told that I couldn't do or be something, so I followed my instincts wherever they led. During college, everything fell into place. I found singing so easy and was always excelling at any type of music I tried. Life flowed with such ease and I found I was always in the right place at the right time. One morning, I was late to my class on music theory. Because this was my least favorite class, I chose the longer way through the school's drama department. As I walked past by the acting classroom, I heard the auditions for the Gilbert and Sullivan operetta *HMS Pinafore*[1]. When the acting director saw me, he called me in for an impromptu audition. I was assigned the lead right away. This type of living with doors of opportunity opened for me continually.

How often does this happen to people? Actually, it happens all the time. There are people all over the world that have experienced the same ease as me and who feel that our world is filled with dreamlike magic. They know that all the opportunities and ease are simply supposed to be. Most people of this sort approach life with immense wonder. None would find it strange to live this way. They, like I was back then, are unconsciously competent. And some are conscious.

I lived in the magic quite happily until I began to listen to the criticisms of others.

My father, for instance, always called me his *flower child* and he said that he did not feel that music was a "real" way to make money. He wanted me married since I would not choose a "real career", and married to a certain type of person. I listened to him because, around the age of thirty-four or thirty-five, I began to think it was time to have a family.

Unfortunately, the marriage that followed included more expectations than magic.

Life became dull. It was filled with volunteering, fake smiles, and endless lunches with other people who were bored and negative. Sure, my husband and I went on marvelous vacations and socialized with all the "right" people—people who had status in our community. But unfortunately, everyone played it safe by asking the same questions and speaking on the same topics of conversation all the time. "Did you see so and so? Wasn't that a great game last night? How are the kids?"

Slowly, the magic slipped away! But, as an unconscious competent, I did not realize I was losing it, until one day, as I was driving and looking at a sunny blue sky dotted with clouds that looked like pretty balls of cotton, it hit me that I wasn't feeling any sense of awe. Heck, I wasn't even grateful.

Where was my wonder? Where was my closeness to the Divine Universe? Where was God? Why could I not hear my soul?

At that moment, I suddenly realized I had lost something extremely special. I asked, "Well, how do I get back to magic?" And this was when I made the decision to find my magic!

I have often wondered why I lost the magic in the first place. Primarily, I think it is because I was supposed to lose it. Why? Well, if I had not lost the magic and lived in what I call the mundaneness of life, I would never have known that living in the magic can be learned. I had to experience not having it to know how it felt and to learn how to get back to my magical life.

There is nothing wrong with living in the mundaneness of life—it's just mundane and ordinary. Life without magic felt heavy to me. Things seemed harder to attain. Goals took longer to achieve. There was little surprise or true fun, and there was a lot of negativity and hardship each day.

In a mundane society, no one looks with wonder at anything. Instead, they expect situations and people to be a certain way. Fear runs rampant in social groups with rigid expectations! It is most important for people who think like this to fit in, be accepted, have the perfect family, the perfect career, and socialize in the ways that are expected and accepted.

But honestly, it doesn't matter what social circle a person travels in, actually. No matter whom we socialize with, in a non-magical life, there is always a level of fitting in with people's expectations. Once in a while, someone tries to step a little out of the conformity. Then, a fear of being different, or of not being successful, or of something else strikes this person and they jump right back into what they have always known and accepted.

I get it! We always want safety, so stepping out into something unknown versus staying with something known and with people who accept you is hard. It is even harder if we don't understand what we will achieve by departing from the herd. By ending our conformity.

The Divine Universe looks for the few who dare to take the journey of belief. Why? Because they are ready to ask the questions, to open themselves to learning, and to trust enough to know it must be better than where they are now. They are eager to step out of "what is supposed to be" and just trust that it will be whatever it turns out to be. And that this is OK.

The Divine Universe looks for the people who feel the breeze and know it is more than a breeze. For those who take the next step with openness, knowing the path will be good. It is looking for the people who dare to be vulnerable and kind because they are beginning to understand that there is more to life than what meets the eye. These people are wanting to discover the magic and become a part of it.

The Divine Universe doesn't want you to fear; it wants you to wonder, love deeply, and keep asking questions—to keep being curious. Because, with wonder and curiosity, you will hear, feel, and discover the magic of your own Universe--of your soul.

Once I realized how much I had lost, I found myself yearning for the magic to return and to be able to talk with my soul. It did not matter what I had to do or learn. I was going to find my way back.

The Divine Universe heard my yearning and it sent teachers, mentors, and situations to help me learn how to hear my soul again. Was the journey hard? No, I did not find it hard because I was discovering more about myself, my life, and what could be. That is not work; it is exploring! It was an exhilarating adventure.

Each step I took left me feeling awake and alive. I sensed it was bringing me one step closer to my destiny. Each step helped me to leave more mundaneness and negativity behind. Each step placed me in the company of interesting and incredible people either teaching me or wanting to learn just like me. I was stepping into a journey of receiving.

I deliberately began my journey to connect to my soul on a new moon because I was beginning a new venture. I hand wrote a letter to Divine Universe and God, which read:

Hello, Divine Universe and my Beloved, I am here to ask that you bring into my life whatever I need to learn so that I can find my way back to you. I am open to receive all the lessons, experiences, and concepts. I am ready!
Thank you and I love you!

I took the letter to the backyard, where I built a fire in my firepit. I read the letter aloud to the sky, and then I burned it and allowed the ashes to soar upwards to the Divine Universe. This was my proclamation and my commitment to follow through with my journey.

Once I had the Beloved and Divine Universe involved in my mission there was no turning back.

SKILLS FOR YOUR JOURNEY

Now that you have experienced a little of my journey, it is your opportunity to take the first step of your journey to know your soul better, using the same tools and skills I just described. You will find similar exercises at the end of every chapter.

The "Skills for Your Journey" sections in this book are designed to help you explore the topics you've just been reading about and practice living in the magic of creation day by day. Each skill or tool is yours to adapt to your own style of learning or experiencing. We are all in this together; however, we learn in different ways. Most importantly, have fun creating.

Grab a pad of paper and a pen, then do the following exercises.

- **Free write about your reasons for reading this book.** Have you had a spiritual wakeup call or moment of awe? Why do you feel that this book may hold the answer you are seeking? Knowing the answers to these questions will help you stay motivated whenever you feel lazy or less enthused.

- **Free write about your desired relationship with your soul.** What intrigues you most about the prospect of living guided by your soul? Write down your answer.
- **Make a commitment to your journey by writing a short letter to the Divine Universe/the Beloved.** Are you ready to be open to all the discovery and growth? Are you open to the experiences and people that the Divine Universe will send to you? (Actually, just in picking up this book it started.)

When you complete your letter, create your own special moment like I did on the new moon with my outdoor fire. You can use my ritual if you like or you can create your own. The important part is your commitment to move forward on this journey until it is complete.

Make the letter as personal as you want. Open your heart. This letter is your opportunity to allow your deepest desires to surface. Enjoy!

Chapter 2
What Is a Soul Connection?

Ah, the freedom of being young, carefree, and always
open to the guidance of something deep within us.

iving through the soul is living as if we are young again.
It takes us back to the innocent age in childhood before
we were told what we could and could not be. An age
before we believed there was only one way to think. Before we
took everything for granted or made worry our partner in life.
When we are young, we are so much freer in thought.

I remember thinking I could be anything. One day I would
decide to become a scientist, and the next, a poet. I was fearless
and would try whatever I felt like trying. My best memories
are those of being with my friends exploring and playing, and
sometimes getting into harmless trouble. We were stretching

our wings, learning about our world and ourselves. Our souls were alive and guiding us.

Every soul comes into the world for a reason—and maybe more than one. Each of us has lessons we are here to learn. Besides helping us learn these personal lessons, our souls also crave three other important things from us. These are their criteria for being happy to be alive within us. Every soul wants to create, expand, and love.

Our souls want us to create—whether that creation is a corporation, a book, pottery, a family, or a community (or all these things). They want us to grow into our potential and expand our wealth, our talents, and our capabilities. They also want us to be supportive and loving to other people, our children, our spouses, our friends, our colleagues, and frankly, anyone we interact with. The purpose of life is to spread our creations and our love and compassion throughout the world.

Our souls love to love. The soul is love because it is the part of us that is directly connected with the light of the Divine Universe—which some people call *heaven.* I am not speaking only of romantic love, but unconditional love and compassion. Universal love for all beings. The untethered soul expresses empathy and kindness, along with greater understanding. But it also understands that each of us is on a unique journey, so there is no need to judge one another. Another's journey is not our journey, and we therefore lack full understanding of it.

Living from a strong connection with the soul means learning how to hear the voice of your soul. Yes, our souls do talk to us—why would they not? Your soul is you. Your true essence is pure, divine light—cosmic energy.

We are within this body, not of this body. The body allows us to live as humans on Earth. Although we sometimes identify with our thoughts and actions and social status and affluence or poverty, we also are not the beliefs we have learned or the things we have or haven't achieved. At the level of our divine essence, we are not parents or children, workers or bosses, women or men (or any other gender configuration). We are the soul, and the soul is us.

Many religions describe how each of us has a soul; however, few people seem confident that they can connect to their souls. Speaking for myself, I hadn't given my soul much thought until the day I heard it speak.

I was driving back from my master gardening course. My instructor had seen one of my gardening designs and told me how much he loved my sense of color, texture, and style. He had asked if I would redo the cottage garden at the extension office. Each county of every state has an agricultural extension office that is linked either to the government or a local university, which supports food growers and landscapers. Ours used the land around it to display different styles of gardening and plants that could be planted in different areas. Master gardeners tend these gardens and take great pride in their creation.

Gardening and design were a hobby I pursued in my leisure hours. I was a musician, not a landscape designer. When my children were still young, I had taken a fancy to creating gardens in our yard at home. My children loved to grab a piece of mint or lemon thyme off a nearby plant as they played with their friends, and I found great peace in planting, combining colors, and watching everything grow. However, doing over a garden that would be viewed by the public—one that was already being managed by a group of very proud women, master gardeners themselves—seemed way out of my league.

My critical monkey mind was having a fit telling me that this was a crazy proposition. *You are not an expert. You do not know what you are doing. These women will hate you.* On and on, the critical mind yelled.

"Enough," I finally said out loud. I just wanted to stop all the noise. As soon as I spoke, peace started to fill my head. Then, I heard a small voice say, "There is no harm in trying. It is all about learning, and maybe the women can be a part of the process, and they will teach you! It really will be fun!"

A smile appeared on my face. This voice was something I could get used to. Yes, why couldn't I just try! If it didn't work out—no harm is done. It could be a lot of fun—this voice was right.

Not only did I accept the job, but I also decided to begin to quiet the harsh, judgmental, and personally degrading loud voice, and instead listen to this soft, positive voice.

At first, quieting that obnoxious voice wasn't fun or easy. My critical mind had grown strong over the years. However, every time I stopped listening to its critical comments and paid attention to the small, supportive voice, I came a step closer to being guided by my soul.

I treated it like a game. When the critical mind started, I pressed an imaginary big red button with my hand and said, "Do over." Then I asked for the quiet, soft voice—my soul's voice—to speak to me. I found that if I concentrated too hard on the voice, then I could not hear it. Even if I could not, pressing the big red button in my imagination and declaring, "Do over," helped me move forward without worry, doubt, or fear. Sometimes a positive, warm, and even humorous thought would pop into my mind spontaneously, and I knew it was my soul's voice talking to me.

It seemed that I would hear my soul whenever I was relaxed, happy, or deeply involved in doing something. If I tried to listen, all I heard was my breathing. I learned that by pushing to hear, I was forming a resistance to the very thing I wanted. But the more I trusted that I would hear the soul when it was ready and relaxed, the more the small voice would enter my ears and mind.

It is regrettable that for us to conform to society, we learn not to trust the inner voice—the sound of the soul. We go from the spiritual "I" of the soul, which is with us when we are born, to the "we " of society; and then, if we want to hear the soul's voice speaking again, we must somehow get back to the "I." For most of us, we must tire of hearing the loud, "I can't" voice before we can allow ourselves to trust the quiet, soft voice.

I began to think about the ways I had conformed to society. In my early years, nothing stood out except my father teaching me that I could do anything; to do what I take on to the best of my ability and not to do anything that would ruin my plans for having what I wanted in life. My core beliefs, which developed during those early years, still serve me well and help me get back to my "I" easier. My dad did an excellent job with teaching me good values and skills in that early period of my life.

When I was in second grade, I hummed while working on my math problems. I instinctively knew that my mind would wander and create stories about all the numbers. I loved the characters I created, which had all the numbers leading incredible lives. I found doing math problems the usual way dull, so it was tough for me to keep my focus without making a game of math. Humming lightly and softly kept me in the present. This was much more fun for me. The only problem was that my teacher hated my light humming. She had the sharp hearing of a cat, so it did not matter where I sat in the classroom—she would zero in on my humming and try to embarrass me.

Though I tried to explain what I was doing to my teacher, she did not want to understand. She did not deem it either normal or acceptable. To please her, I had to forgo what I knew inside was right for me and conform to what she said was good for me. No humming! No stories!

My focus waned, and my grade in math went down.

How many kids have had similar experiences in school? How many of us override the wisdom of our souls for the sake of fitting in? You see, the teacher only wanted me to do my work in math like everyone else. This is conformity! Her attitude was: "Do what must be done; however, do it as I, the teacher (or parent, or others) deem it should be done." To achieve her goal of having me do math like everyone else, my teacher chose to embarrass me. Shame was her weapon to pressure me to conform to her desire. Thus, what could have been a wonderful lesson on how to help yourself focus on a task that requires concentration, which probably would have helped three-quarters of the class so much that our grades would have gone up, was not. Instead, the teacher gained a frustrated student.

Conformity, in a nutshell, is being the same. Conformists don't rock the boat.

The even bigger lesson of compliance is that we are forced to agree that some authority figure outside of us knows what is better for us.

This denial of the soul is HUGE! By learning to trust that a source outside us is more correct or desirable to society than our inner source we give up on the soul. In conformity, we become the "we" and lose the "I."

The voice of "I," the soul, at this point, becomes quiet.

After passing a course to be a master gardener, I was invited to be a master gardener at the agricultural extension office. This was an honor. I was to join some of the best master gardeners as they created, groomed, and grew wonderful display gardens for the public to see different styles of gardens. I was asked to join the "cottage garden" group. All of the masters in this group were good friends and set in their ideas of style, type of plants, and formation of the cottage garden.

When the extension office director decided the cottage garden needed a facelift, he asked me to design a new design for the cottage garden. This created an upheaval with the members of the garden. How dare he ask the newcomer—me—to change a garden they had cared over for fifteen years. What would I know that they did not already know? Why was I the chosen one? These and many other critical questions were asked.

No one would have blamed me for backing down from the opportunity to have my design displayed at a well-respected extension if they had heard the critical comments and felt the anger these master gardeners expressed to me. I received phone calls and cold shoulders. It would have been easy for me to let the opportunity go and conform to the group. Let go of all myself to blend in as the new kid and just enjoy doing my little bit to beautify an established garden. Conformity would be easy, but would it be enough? I had a real knack for color and texture combination. I also had done a lot of research on the cottage gardens in England for my own yard. Designing the extensions office cottage garden would be incredibly fun for me and I knew it would be the prettiest garden on display.

The question was clear: Should I live in conformity with the community and not rock the boat, do what was expected, and play the part of the newbie, or should I accept what I knew I was good at and bring the garden to the height it was always meant to be? I took time that night to sit under my favorite tree in my backyard and drink a cup of tea. This was my sacred place, my place to dream and create worlds. As I sat there sipping away, I thought, *Maybe there is a way to get the members of the garden on board with what the extension office wants. Do I have to design this garden alone? Yes, I could. However, wouldn't it be more fun and beneficial to include everyone in the new design? Didn't these wonderful caretakers of this garden for years deserve to be part of this process?* I then knew what I had to do.

The next day I called all the gardeners to a meeting to discuss the design and together, we designed the most wonderful cottage garden ever seen in our community.

When we open up to our talents and gifts, we are opening to our "I" because our talents and gifts are part of our soul. As a little girl of three years of age I would turn my baby doll crib on its side, set up all my dolls and stuffed animals looking at my standing crib and begin to teach.   What was really interesting was that I was teaching about spirit and God.   I was in "I" of my soul. When we trust our gifts and talents, we discover our true abilities and gain a strong confidence from the soul itself. Through genuine connection to our "I" /soul, we can form stronger cooperative communities. Cooperation does not have to mean sacrificing our capacity for independent thought.

As I explored my "I" in projects like the one at the cottage garden, I regained something that I had lost over the years. Previously, by trying to fit into the world I found myself living in, I had allowed myself to lose my "I" and lost the foundation of my sense of identity. Who I was and what I felt was right for me were unknown to me. This had opened the door for society at large, my parents, my teachers, my peers, and anyone else with an opinion to influence the directions of my life and define my choices and behavior.

I already knew that the rules of conformity I had internalized as a child were failing me. What I had been taught and what I felt that I was expected to do with my life was not what the hidden "I" wanted or was happy about. Conforming to expectations, I had married a man who was "perfect on paper." I thought for a time that I had "made it." However, both he and I were conforming to our families' desires for us at the expense of any personal desires or dreams on our own parts.

For me to find my inner divine, my soul, and hear its soft, loving voice meant getting back in touch with my "I." My "I" is my soul. Your "I" is yours.

The soft voice of the soul is the voice of all creation and growth. It is our link to the divine light and the Divine Universe. It is free of limitations because it knows better, and it also knows that it doesn't have to conform to any expectations because it is part of everything ever created and holds the potential to transform.

My soul knows why I am here. It knows what I am here to become. Only my soul understands its evolution and the lessons it needs to learn. It understands the possibilities and creations it can create. And it is connected to the Divine Universe and the Beloved.

And your soul knows your potential, your evolution, and your life lessons. And it is also connected to the Divine Universe and the Beloved.

That means that when any of us opens to our soul, we are opening to the Divine Universe. This Divine Universe creates through us. We are a big part of the Universe. Our souls are links between us, living on Earth, and the whole vast cosmos— links to everything that ever was, is, and ever shall be. We are open to expanding and growing because our souls came here to evolve. Without our personal growth, there would be no evolution.

The loving, positive voice inside each of us is the voice of new possibilities and ideas, and sincere belief in ourselves and the Universe. One voice serves for all. The voice of the soul is never judgmental, critical, or harsh. It is always nurturing, positive, funny, adventurous, and loving.

If and when we begin to live by our soul, we, indeed, do have everything we need to live, grow, create, love, and thrive. Everything we need is right inside us because our soul is the direct connection to Source/Beloved God.

Being connected to the Beloved is not a farfetched concept. Philosophers of our ancient world understood this powerful connection. Religions use the word *omnipresent* meaning "everywhere" to describe the Beloved's location. The Beloved/God is omnipresent—in every tree, animal, blade of grass, drop of water, molecule of air we breathe, and in each of our souls.

Coming back to "I" may sound selfish. However, it is in regaining ourselves so that we can open to our soul, to Spirit and all life. Starting again at "I," like little children, also helps us to see the wonder, the curiosity, and the magnificence of our world and to realize how very much we are part of our vast cosmos and heaven.

If I wanted to connect to my soul completely, I had to begin to understand my "I." Who was this "I"? What were her (at least I thought it was a her) dreams or desires? What was she about? What did she want for me on this planet?

It stood to reason that if I was my soul then beginning to open myself to myself was opening myself to my "I"/soul. The best way I found to begin this process was to honor myself.

Honoring myself sounded so self-centered in my head when I thought about doing it, however, it was completely the opposite in action. I began by listening to my body. When my stomach felt funny, I would stop and ask myself, *Why?* Then I would address whatever needed to be addressed. If I felt sad or angry, I didn't push down the emotions. Instead, I would ask myself what was wrong, *Why am I angry?*

I watched what I was eating, listened to on the radio, reading on social networks, and watching on TV to observe how it was affecting me—and avoided things that had an adverse impact. I also noticed how I felt around others. This last was very freeing.

My father used to call me the Little Diplomat, meaning I could smooth over any disagreements. I made everyone feel at home. Now, I was to give myself freedom to not fix the conversation or other people's feelings. But instead to see how I felt about the dynamic. I could let things play out the way they were supposed to. I also made time to just be, to meditate, and to exercise. I found that I had been putting up with people who were taking from me—taking my time, energy, happiness, and possibilities.

Why had I allowed this in the past? Because it was the norm?

As I became more comfortable with my "I," those people left me before I could say anything. I think they felt the difference too.

Everyone else's needs had been overriding my own for quite a while. Not just my children's needs—which, of course, are a mother's responsibility to a certain extent, especially when her kids are too young to care for themselves—but the needs of grown people. No wonder I had been so tired and grouchy.

It makes sense that if we are not feeling well we can't spread goodness. I had been running on empty for some time. Now that I was honoring myself and taking the time to refuel, I found I was more present with my kids and more in touch with being in the present moment. What fun it was and gave me a nice feeling of freedom. I think that was because my critical monkey mind had begun to be a little quieter.

Honoring myself turned into much more of a discovery than I originally thought it would be. I found that the more I honored myself, the more I honored others in my life. I was making more time for them and always gave them my full attention when we were together. I also found people responding in incredible ways to this treatment. There was much more laughter and heart-to-heart talks. I was really listening, so people were able to open themselves to me. My old friendships where deepening and the new friends I was bonding with were amazing.

As I honored myself and my life, my "I" began sending little urges. It was as if it was lighting a fire deep in me to try new things. I began to ride my bike again, which was very meaningful because when I was young my bike and I were inseparable. I also found myself dancing around the house—so fun. Sometimes I would take a drive to somewhere random, finding antique stores or unique sights along the way, and maybe grabbing an ice cream cone.

One morning, I woke with the strong urge to write again. I had written poetry in high school. So, I went to a coffee shop and started journaling. That one visit to write turned into two and three, until soon writing in a coffee shop was filling my whole morning every day. Little did I know that my soul's urge was to write a book.

When I finally felt the "I" becoming more "me" and I had gained awareness of how I had been giving my power away to outside forces, I felt the need to conform and my worries about what others thought of me leave me. Wow, does it ever feel good to take the pressure off. The fear of trying things outside my normal routine was gone.

Most of all, I enjoyed how my perception on creating and being changed. What a lot of time, energy, and space in my head I had wasted on trying to conform, keep to the rules, and be acceptable. Now, with all that mental noise gone, I could finish my book with ease, be with whomever I chose to be with, and just love being myself.

I was ready to learn the skills and open myself up to my soul completely. Little did I realize what the Divine Universe had in store for me: a lesson in how to say good-bye to my critical mind.

Are you ready to silence yours?

SKILLS FOR YOUR JOURNEY

Now that you have experienced a little of my journey to honor myself more, it is your opportunity to take similar steps. Try these two activities.

- **Make today a daydream day!** Take time to think back to the fun of your childhood. Remember the good times when you were uninhibited and had the confidence, bravery, and openness of mind to try new things. Remember feeling free while you swung high on a swing or rode your bike fast down the hill with no hands. My, how brave you were!

- As kids, we trusted something bigger than us to keep us safe. Everything was an experiment. Our days were always filled with wonder. Can you remember the joy you felt when you played with friends or your excitement when you rode your bike for the first time? That feeling is the feeling of living with your soul. Enjoy the daydream day and use it to reignite that same feeling of possibility inside you again.

- **Figure out what you want.** What are you looking for in life? What are you hoping to achieve? And why is this important to you? Take out a piece of paper. Write down what you are looking for in your life and in yourself. Allow yourself to write openly without holding back. The more honest we are with ourselves, the more we can accept who we are. An honestly expressed desire is a good place to start.

    Everything you need is within you. This exercise is a great way to begin looking for it.

Chapter 3

The Magic Is in the Stillness

All awareness and growth begin and end with the
discovery of the inner-self—the true you!

Most of us lead busy lives. The idea of taking time to do nothing does not sound fun or like something most of us would enjoy doing. Why is this? Because even when we are relaxing, we are still doing. We are either watching a movie, reading a book or magazine, or looking at posts on social media or YouTube. The idea of just sitting still with ourselves while allowing our thoughts to drift sounds hard and foreign for most of us.

However, growth of awareness happens in the quiet—this is the domain of the inner self, the place of timelessness, creativity, love, greater understanding, and truth. Of all the tools

I will introduce you to in this book, meditation is probably one of the most important.

Reading this assertion, you may already be thinking, *Yes Alena, I realize how everyone loves meditation. But not me. I just can't seem to shut off my mind or sit that long or find the time to meditate, and so on.* The excuses are endless. I used to feel the same resistance to meditation.

When I first began meditating, I had the hardest time sitting silent and still in a group. I found myself starting to giggle—often at the most inconvenient times. I especially found the traditional Hindu meditation, where you are sitting with legs crossed, a straight back, and uttering, "Om," seemed foreign and difficult. But the more I practiced, the more I loved it.

Meditation has opened up my world in ways that I would never have imagined possible a few years ago. Once I learned how to focus my mind through meditation, the capacity to focus helped me be more effective in every part of my life. I even learned how to relax all my muscles by just saying one phrase: "Be still my heart!"

During my divorce, my former husband and I had to go to court many times. The courtroom held a very heavy, ego-driven energy that made me physically ill whenever I entered it. The worst part, as you can probably imagine, was when I had to be on the stand, testifying. The lawyers working for my husband were cruel. But it was not what they said that rattled me. One lawyer would roll his eyes or wave me away whenever I answered a question. However, he was careful to ensure that the judge never saw any of this disrespectful behavior. Already nervous to the point of feeling nauseated, I would become confused by his questions and his dismissal of my replies. It made the whole experience that much more fraught.

My reaction to the lawyers wasn't going to help my children and me. I had to learn how to function in this situation. Teaching me to perform well under pressure is where my soul shone.

One day, as I sat relaxed in my car at a stoplight, my soul said, "You can be this relaxed in the courtroom if you just train your body to be."

This idea was brilliant! I decided to choose the phrase "Be still my heart" from the book *As a Man Thinketh* by James Allen[2]. Every time I said it, I would breathe deeply, and relax my body. I would practice in my meditation room twice a day. And when driving to and from my errands as I was landscaping gardens around town or transporting my kids to school and afterschool activities, I practiced saying the phrase and thoroughly relaxing at every stoplight. It took only a week and a half to create a positive, meditative trigger that I could activate in an instant with one mental prompt on an exhalation of air.

The next time I had to take the stand in court, I was calm, focused, and centered. No more could the lawyers rattle or confuse me. No more did I allow the energy of the room to create negative feelings in me. I was in my divine inner self, my soul, and it was in me.

There Are Many Ways to Meditate

The good news is that there is a type of meditation that suits everyone's personal style and preferences.

Ancient philosophers and life teachers, such as Zen masters and the Buddha, all advocated the use of meditation for achieving flow, calmness, and access to higher dimensions. Among these traditions is Taoism, which divides meditation into three categories: meditations for concentration, visualization, and insight.

In Buddhism, meditation is divided into two categories: calm, stabilizing meditation (śamatha), and observational, analytical meditation (*vipassana*).

All religions and modalities for self-mastery incorporate a type of meditation or prayer in their practices, and many of these meditations involve the use of mantras—repetitively spoken or chanted words that focus the mind. I was raised in the Catholic faith, which uses a rosary—a circle of differently shaped beads along with a medallion and a cross—to facilitate prayers and intentions. Each bead has a particular prayer assigned to it. The repetition of the prayers is a mantra, as the people performing them allow their minds to clear through concentrating on the words of the prayer.

These are but a small handful of meditation practices. And, in reality, meditating is not so foreign for most of us. We have always had a type of meditation in our lives. In fact, you may find it to be not only easy but liberating. Nothing feels better than freeing our minds of all obligation, worry, demands of the day, timetables, and fear. During meditation, we feel timeless yet present, empty yet complete. We start to see and understand what is real and begin to bring this feeling into everyday life. We naturally become calmer, develop our capacities for listening deeper and understanding several sides of an issue, and gain a greater understanding of purpose and life in general.

When I finally could quiet my mind enough to sit in my meditation group without giggling, I found that meditation was where I received answers to my seemingly endless questions about what was happening to my family and me during my divorce. The more I began to accept my situation through the meditative process, the more I opened to a greater understanding. I was now able to raise myself above the situation. It is like the old saying, "Rise above the forest to see the best way out." At last, I was able to see the best way to obtain a good outcome for everyone involved. Peace and stillness filled my mind and heart. Meditation brought me welcome relief and has changed the way I deal with the obstacles in my life ever since.

Throughout my search for my style of meditating, I came across many wonderful guided and unguided meditation practices. I also studied Transcendental Meditation, mindfulness, and Taoist meditation. All were wonderful and had something special in them; still, my monkey mind would eventually creep in and disturb me. The one that ultimately helped me conquer my busy mind issue was the shamanic practice of journeying. Journeying is precisely what it sounds like: traveling to another realm of existence.

Each time I journey, I am guided to something bigger than myself and transported to another world. On journeys, I meet my spiritual guides and visit incredible places in other times and more. My very first journey, for example, was to meet my older self. The advice I received from this older version of me was eye-opening. Ever since I discovered journeying, I have been able to meditate anytime I feel the need.

I meditate right when I get up. I do a short, beautiful meditation with the intention: "How may I best serve today?"

A second meditation in the afternoon during my afternoon energy lull brings me into a deepness. In the past, I used to try to boost my energy with caffeine or exercise. Nothing worked well. However, meditation is perfect. Sometimes, because my energy just wants to slip into that wonderful, peaceful, timelessness that meditation usually takes me to, I receive some of the best meditative gifts ever during afternoon meditations. Because I am easily in the sleepy state in the late afternoon, my journey meditations are filled with incredible detail and information. My guide takes me to see angels, parallel universes, or even other guides or teachers.

One time I asked, *If my Beloved God is omnipresent, wouldn't that mean the Beloved is inside me?* My guide took me to an incredible land of pure light. As I stood next to a glistening waterfall, a figure of pure light walked over to me. Before I knew it, this figure was inside me, then outside me and then, back inside me. I heard very clearly, *"By Spirit, I flow in and out of you all the time. I am always with you."* This meditation, in particular, changed my whole perception of the Beloved God. No more did I see an old man with a white beard sitting on a throne in heaven. Now, I see this powerful, loving force filling me and all life around me—every day. The Beloved is in the trees, the water, and the wind.

You really owe it to yourself to open to the experience. The only requirement for me to be successful with meditation is consistency in trying. Some days I have wow meditations. Others, it seems like I have ants in my pants and just can't sit still. So be it. These are the days I step outside or go to a nature center and feel life. I talk to the trees and whatever else comes to me. The calmness of nature becomes my calm. Most of the time, I receive messages or clarity. This makes sense because it is a type of meditation and the Beloved is fully present in every breath I take. It is the continual doing—being present when I am walking in nature or creating sacredness in my private space by sitting, breathing, relaxing, and just being—that matters. Through consistency, my practice has grown to be a powerful feature of my life.

Establishing a Sacred Space or Sanctuary

Although I love being in nature and taking many meditative walks, I also wanted to be able to enjoy a deep, seated meditation and experience the everything-and-nothing space, a "sweet spot" that everyone in my meditation group had spoken about which sounded enticing. To support myself in my endeavor to experience that deep state, I created a sacred space in my home in a room seldom used by the family that has three beautiful windows through which I could see and feel the nature in my gardens. I decorated this sanctuary with my favorite antique furniture and added some candles, and it was perfect.

There was only one problem: my busy "monkey" mind. This is what the Buddhists call thoughts that jump around and distract us. I loved the space, but I could not quiet my mind long enough to enter deep meditation. If this was my sacred space—a space for me to feel free to be and discover more about who I wanted to be and to seek peace when the outside world was so noisy and unsettling—how could I keep the world at bay?

A wonderful Wiccan friend of mine once was told to put a protective white light around myself whenever I felt the need for sanctuary. It occurred to me that I could put a white light around my sacred space to seal it off from external influences and allow me to have a quiet mind. I stood outside my room and drew a white light circle around the room. That was energetically helpful. But something was still missing. If my monkey mind was a part of me, then how could I put it outside the white circle? Why couldn't I take a break from this part of my mind? Was that even possible?

I stood outside my circle and said, "Worry, doubt, and fear shall not enter here!" With a gentle whoosh of my hand, I pushed the worry, doubt, and fear into an imaginary box and put it up on a shelf. "Now stay there for five minutes while I am in my sacred space," I commanded before stepping inside. *Ahhh . . . peace!*

Once I could be in my sacred place for five minutes, I lengthened the time to ten, then fifteen minutes. Soon I was able to be in my sacred space meditating or anything else I wanted to do in my space without my critical monkey mind interrupting.

The sacred space ritual of leaving the negativity outside the circle of white light is a powerful way for us to begin to control our thoughts. I never want negativity to pollute my space. If I have a negative thought or series of negative thoughts while I am meditating, I say, "No, Leave from the circle." I then clap my hands to interrupt the energy and push it out of the circle. The result is an immediate cessation of negative thought and a soothing feeling of tranquility.

A place that you designate as your own, where you can have peace and grow, is freeing. Most beneficial is leaving any negativity you feel outside that space. A sacred space serves two primary purposes. The first of these is to give us a safe place to be, grow, and discover a beautiful sense of inner divinity. The second is to help us train our minds in detachment. Once we have tasted freedom from the busyness and criticalness of the monkey mind, we begin to crave even more freedom—and this is found in detachment from outside desires and thoughts.

I love my sacred space. It is my place to dream, gain greater insight and knowledge, and discover new facets of the Divine. Sometimes, it is a place just to relax and be myself. Visualize white light around your space and furnish it with belongings that have beauty or special significance for you to personalize it, and I'm sure you'll come to love yours just as much. You'll love how you feel when you spend time with your divine soul.

SKILLS FOR YOUR JOURNEY

Now it is your turn. If you already meditate, perhaps exploring some of the methods I have written about will bring you to a new level of wholeness in your life. If you are just beginning to meditate, yay. Congratulations. A vast world awaits you.

Meditation is one of the very best ways to find out that spiritual awareness and growth begin and end with the true inner self—your soul.

- **Walk in nature while being present.** Listen to everything around you for patterns or uniqueness of sound. Maybe you will hear a bird singing and a chipmunk chewing wood, and a breeze rustling as it plays with the grass or trees. Nature is presenting a peaceful symphony just for you!

  Next, you may even begin to receive and feel messages from the natural world around you. For example, one time I was having such a bad day that I wasn't sure how I would keep going. So, I allowed my car to take me and eventually I found myself at a stone fence leading up a drive on a hill. I followed the stone fence to the top of the large hill to find an old monastery. The trees beside it were old and majestic. I parked and got out of my car and sat down in a clearing between these trees, where I closed my eyes, and surrendered everything to the Beloved God. Right at that moment a soft breeze kissed my cheek. With my eyes still closed, I felt as if the trees were leaning in on me. I opened my eyes to see insects walking in a circle around me, and I heard the caw of a bird above. Looking up, I saw a beautiful hawk circling me. The whole world of nature was telling me I was heard and not alone. The Beloved God had sent me these messengers to show me that everything is "one." It all comes from one source.

- **Establish a sacred space in your home.** If you are someone who likes structure, you can establish a permanent sacred space specially designated for meditation and self-discovery. Remember, this space is your space. Decorate it with whatever you love. If it is a place in nature, be sure it is a space that calls to you.

  You can also establish temporary sacred spaces. I tend to travel quite often, so I have acquired a shawl-type blanket that I bring on each trip. I lay this shawl on the bed in every hotel room I enter to make that bed my sacred space temporarily. Try it for yourself. You can also make a chair you plan to sit in for a while a sacred space.

  Before you enter your sacred space, remember to put a white light around it. Start drawing the white light with your finger from the north and go clockwise to east, south, west, and back to the north. Say something that works for you to begin clearing the mind and energy of your body while you visualize yourself pushing the negative energy away from your sacred space and white light. An example would be, "No worry, doubt, or fear shall enter here" or "I enter with a clear mind to replenish and discover my inner world." Or make up your own. The important thing is to say something to prepare your intention that leaves the critical business of the world outside your sacred space.

- **Discover your preferred style of meditation.** There are many different ways to meditate, and it can be fun to try out all of them. Each has something different to offer. Keep your mind open and enjoy the process of discovery. Some ways will be more effective than others for you. When you find a meditation that is perfect for your needs, it feels like home.

Here's a quick and easy meditation you can do anywhere anytime. I learned this mini meditation from a Taoist master. It is perfect for when I feel scattered or a little stressed, or even if I simply need to calm down with kids or in traffic. The best part is that it is short and centers me, enabling me to quickly access the sweet spot in meditation. This is an incredible feeling of timelessness and centeredness, with a sense of all-peaceful-everythingness-and-nothingness. You'll know it when you experience it, I promise.

Relax with three deep breaths. When you have opened your abdomen with the breath in this way, allow yourself to continue to breathe while concentrating on the space between your in-breath and out-breath. Exhalation should simply be a release of air.

Isn't it absolutely the most peaceful space?

Meditation is the most powerful gift you can give yourself. It is a gift that will continue to give as long as you grow with it. The time I devote to meditation in the morning has become one of my favorite times of the day. It is an excellent place to connect with my soul. Find the time that works best for you, and I am sure you will have a comparable experience. Also remember, all awareness and growth begin and end with discovery of your divine inner self—the true you!

Chapter 4
You Are Worth It!

*Until I see the worthiness of myself—my own beauty—I will
not understand how to see worthiness in anyone else.*

There is a passage from Lao Tzu's *Tao Te Ching* that opened
my eyes to how important each of us is to one another
and, potentially, to everyone in the world. Here is my
contemporary interpretation of the Master's words.

> *Because you believe in yourself,*
> *You don't try to convince others.*
> *Because you are content with yourself,*
> *You don't need others' approval.*
> *Because you accept yourself,*
> *The whole world accepts you[4].*

When I was eighteen years old, I began to study the works of Wayne Dyer, Ed.D. I read his books on human potential and allowed myself to become engrossed in everything he espoused and practiced. In all truth, I actually started to study him so I could understand why so many people were sad or angry, and why so many, including my parents, would push their beliefs on me. Later in Dr. Dyer's career he studied *Tao Te Ching*, a book about the philosophy known as Taoism[4]. *Tao Te Ching*, traditionally credited to sixth-century BCE Chinese philosopher Lao Tzu. The Tao means "the Way[4]." I find it to be a neverending resource on understanding a way to flow, trust, and be with the Universe instead of fighting or resisting against it. The followers of this belief system are called Taoists. One practice the Taoists have is a meditation to disperse blocks. I have had a lot of success with it and find it easy as well as effective.

This philosophy is a way to live closer to the Beloved God. Because Dr. Dyer was studying the *Tao Te Ching* and practicing its principles, I began to read and study it too[3].

Once I was on my journey to connect and live by my soul, I felt an urge to read Lau Tzu's book again. Reflecting on these words, sent me on the next important step of my journey of living with my soul. I found myself reading the book over and over.

My journey's first two steps taught me the importance of honoring my mind, body, and soul. They made me powerfully aware of the importance of treating myself well. As I treated myself with greater respect and care, I was able to hear the voice of my intuition better, and able to discern which actions either helped me grow or limited my growth.

And I loved the new mental and emotional freedom I felt as a result of developing a regular practice of meditation and shamanic journeying.

The powerful passage from *Tao Te Ching* that I just shared with you prompted me to ask, *Do I believe in myself?*[4] And the answer was a heartfelt yes! I did believe in my ability to achieve my goals in life.

But was I content with myself? Sometimes I was incredibly hard on myself. A loud, critical voice was there every time I made a mistake or things didn't turn out as I wanted, saying, *Well, what did you think would happen? You know better than to . . . !*

I heard this critical voice when I was starting my business and when I was finishing my first book. Starting a business takes a considerable amount of time. There is building the structure of the business, branding, creating content, marketing—so there was much I needed to learn and implement. During this period, I was a newly single parent of three boys who were used to having their mom at their disposal at all times, day and night. I felt a degree of guilt for not always being available right when my children wanted my attention.

I took steps to create a structured schedule and separate my family time with my kids from my work time with my business activities. All would go well for a while, but then, if I suffered a minor setback or did something larger to create the income I needed for my family, wow, my critical monkey mind would chime in to feed me thoughts of guilt and to shame me. *You are wasting your time and losing time with your children. Why are you allowing this business to take you away from being a mom? Your kids need you, and you are off galivanting! This business is too hard for you right now. Wait until the boys are grown and then see what happens.*

Now I can look back at these comments and tell that they come from my critical monkey mind. They always sounded like a little Italian grandmother in my head. But while I was living through that period in my life, this internal criticism would instantly throw me into feelings of being a bad mom because I was "not putting my family foremost" and only giving them my attention. I would shroud myself with the guilt and the shame I felt.

If I had given in to the dictates of my critical "mother monkey" mind, it could have led me to disband a business that now helps thousands of people.

I realize I am not the only one who has heard these types of comments ringing in their ears. It is funny how the critical monkey mind is ready and waiting to strike us just when we are the most vulnerable, like times when we already feel bad or a little unsure about what is happening and our ability to create it.

For me, when I heard the criticism, although I genuinely felt I could achieve anything if I set my mind to it, I just couldn't make a mistake or else the critical mind would take over my thoughts. There was a thin line I apparently didn't like crossing over.

This same passage from *Tao Te Ching* instructs us to believe in and accept ourselves whether the chips are high or the chips are low.[4] Reading it, I felt urged to be content with myself—not just the me that everyone loves and adores, but *me* in my totality. I wanted to accept my incredible soul as my guide in life. To do that, I understood that I have to accept the person I am!

I personally call the phase of learning to accept myself the "It's okay" part of my journey. This is because I found myself saying, "It's okay" every time the critical voice would pounce on me like a hungry lion jumping out at me from behind a bush.

Learning to accept and honor myself in all my aspects brought me tremendous relief. As I did, I was able to let go of the immense pressure I put on myself to be the kind of woman I thought others would accept or expected me to be. Once I let go of this pressure, I realized how much it had weighed on me and limited my options.

It was because of this pressure that I had allowed others to tell me how to live, which took me off my path. Because I had never realized how much that pressure was weighing me down, I had allowed my lack of trust in myself to rob me of the magic in my life.

It was okay not to be the "perfect" mom! In all seriousness there is no such thing as "perfect." I felt so light once the pressure to be perfect was gone. I had much more fun with my children and with myself. Letting go of a weird expectation allowed me to be more of myself with my kids. And because our time together was so much fun and our relationships so genuine and open then, when we were apart, and I was working on my business I was able to be fully present with it too. The heaviness of my critical mind was gone in both places.

Letting go of being perfect was a humongous step for me. But in addition to this, it is also important for us to know and feel that we are enough. For me, it was only after dropping an expectation of perfection that I was able to begin to really accept and even love myself.

When I was living as an unconscious competent and the magic was active in my life every day, I trusted the Beloved/ the Universe. This was easy to do because I was getting good results. Everyone around me thought I was confident—and I was, for the most part. Even so, there was always a little bit of fear that I wasn't actually "enough." Because of this I always felt I had to try harder and work harder to prove I was worthy of the gifts I was receiving.

I was making a living in a career my family disapproved of. Although I did very well at it, how much more could I have achieved if I had really accepted myself and my dreams, and had more belief in the value of my life and choices? Who would I have ended up marrying if I had accepted myself fully?

I had allowed other peoples and societies beliefs, criticisms, and expectations to pollute my mind, body, and soul. It was time to clean out my mind—to get rid of the pollution altering my choices—and finally be free to accept me as me!

In meditation, I asked, *Is it too late for me to begin this part of the journey?*

My soul answered quickly, "This is as good of a time as any."

I have come to know this stage as a continuation of my journey as the return to my "I" in its purest form. I feel immense gratitude that I took the necessary steps to cleanse my mind, body, and soul and become whole in myself. This detoxification has allowed the space and clarity to see the real me. Today, all facets of me are present. I have come back to my "I" or first chakra, eased out the false beliefs (at least the ones to my knowledge) and discovered my true talents and gifts. I have also discovered and come to accept both my *masculine*, which is the doing or action-taking part of me, and the feminine, which is the introspective part of me. I used to be focused on the doing part of me – the masculine. Sometimes focusing only on. The masculine had me spinning in circles, listening too much to outside sources and their demands . These sources included parents, teachers, my job, media, even my husband and children. Now I am opening more to my feminine part of my "I" which is more of the quiet introspective side of me. Many of the things I love most about myself are feminine traits, including some qualities that I have come to see as strengths which I used to consider faults. I am whole and happy now because I let my soul guide me.

The path I took has cleared the way for my soul—my inner light—to shine brighter. These days, I laugh freely. I also sometimes will call people out on actions or words they say that hurt them or others. However, I do this with such love and joy that we both laugh together. In these simple exchanges, I help them to accept themselves a little more for being as they really are.

If I hadn't become fully whole in my "I," then I would never be able to show others that it is okay for them to accept their own. I wouldn't even have known what that meant.

Learning to Be All of You

One good belief I hold is: *If I am going to do something, then I must do it!*

Once I made the decision to begin the process of unpolluting myself and to accept, even love, all of myself, I jumped right to treating myself as the sacred soul I am.

I found the process fascinating on the conceptual level. What was it to *treat yourself as sacred?* What did the term *sacred* even mean? Over time, I found out that treating myself as sacred is as important as learning to talk or walk.

Treating ourselves as sacred and honoring ourselves are overlapping, yet slightly different things. They definitely work together.

To honor yourself means respecting who you are. It means listening to your body and your mind and your soul to assess their current condition and your needs.

Honoring yourself also requires you to find out what works for you. How do you like to live? Whose company do you thrive in? It opens the door for you to discover the real you and what makes you tick.

I love thinking about all those questions and making observations that bring me answers.

To treat yourself as sacred means clearing your mind, body, and spirit of anything that is not good for you now or for the person you want to evolve into—ridding yourself of what doesn't serve you..

It also means only allowing yourself to receive the best and giving yourself the best. The *best* being everything that helps you grow in love.

Honoring yourself takes on a powerful significance when you pair it with the sacredness of your "I."

When I arrived at this stage of my journey, I began by making a list of ways to treat myself with sacredness and honor myself. I made three columns at the top of a piece of paper and labeled them Body, Mind, and Soul. Then I asked myself a bunch of questions, such as, *How am I honoring my body today? Do I listen to things that feed my mind or drag me down? How can I begin to nourish my spirit?* I answered myself as honestly as possible. The next morning, I began using my answers as the basis of various self-assessments. I began to gather data so that I could clean anything out of my environment that did not serve my sacred self.

Because this idea and practice was so new to me, I started slowly. I began first with my body. When I awoke, I asked my soul how I could best serve my body that day and checked in with my physical sensations. How was my body feeling? Assessment: Sleepy!

Based on this information, I allowed myself to move slowly and have a cup of tea before doing my morning yoga regimen. To my amazement, my body responded much better during practice than usual. As I moved through the poses in my regimen, I allowed anything stored in my muscles and joints to release and let go—sacredly clearing toxins from my system. I felt clear and alive. My body responded well to this approach of honoring how it was feeling and easing it into doing activity. The sacred clearing created an air of freshness and gave me a sense of a new beginning.

When I was out at a lunch meeting that same day, I felt more at ease. As I drove to lunch, I noticed myself thinking, *What are we going to accomplish?* Then I shifted to looking at myself as sacred and as who I am in my best and purest form. I let go of the intention to do something, took a breath, and filled my heart with love. While I was at lunch, I let go of any feeling of "having to chat." I didn't push myself to speak with my colleagues. Although my intention to interact verbally was gone, I still was communicating with everyone at the table—just more organically and authentically. The lunch was so much more fun and real than I had anticipated it being and I learned more about the others present than I ever had before.

Driving home, I found myself going back over lunch and reviewing the conversations and meanings. My critical voice chimed in, ruing the otherwise beautiful experience. Noticing this, I took action to shift it.

Why was I allowing myself to second guess what had felt so fun and good? This was learned pollution in my head. It was not sacred and would not help me evolve to be my best. I turned on a podcast about French country décor, a hobby of mine. That was much more fun, so I was happy again.

Each time I honored and treated myself sacredly with my feelings or desires on that day, I found it was actually not affecting anyone other than me. And the effect on me was profound! I was relaxed and actually enjoying everything I was experiencing so much more than usual. I was really listening and intently present to my life. Even though I was focusing on myself and my body's responses and my feelings, it seemed to improve my relationships with others and improve the situations we were in. In honoring my body and allowing it to be my sacred domain, I wasn't trying to be someone else or do what I thought others expected me to do.

During the second week of honoring/sacredness, I stopped rushing around like a crazy person. I wondered, *Why do I rush around? Why do I have to feel productive?* It made much more sense to be calm and think things through thoroughly. By the end of that week, I saw major changes in myself. I had a new respect for myself and the way I conducted my life. I was listening to my body, allowing myself to feel, and trusting the feelings I felt. And I was working through the old beliefs and habits and getting rid of anything not treating me or my life sacred. There was no more pushing feelings down or just doing or being something I was not.

As a result of removing the pressure and slowing down, I began to really like myself! I made a point to congratulate myself if I did something I liked, and I felt comfortable being me.

No more did someone else's bad day affect me. I would not allow it.

I now made time to "just be" with myself in my sacred space. I didn't rush through the time I spent there, either. Instead I would light my candles, treat it as a sacred moment, sit, breathe, and enjoy. I noticed that my meditations that week were deeper than before and filled with greater insight.

What I found was that I really liked myself. I was alright! And I liked the feeling of liking myself. A solid, calm, strong confidence was growing inside my belly. This was a new feeling and one I hadn't really thought would happen. Trust! I truly was starting to trust myself to know what was good for me. Gone was the effort to be something for someone else or to prove anything. Gone was people-pleasing and the worry that someone wasn't pleased with me. Their approval was not important, and, as I subsequently learned, people's expectations always had more to do with them than they did me.

More and more I knew what was good for me, and my trust in my thoughts and feelings grew. The more insightful I grew about my feelings, the more drawn to me people were. It was as if they knew and could feel the calm center and inner knowing I was developing.

The results I got from honoring my body helped me to open up to my soul. Why would I want to hear criticism of myself? Why would I want to hear that I couldn't do something? My critical monkey mind became much quieter than it ever had been before.

This was big for me because it was helping me to move forward into starting to accept all of myself, even my so-called faults. My honoring and sacredness were propelling me forward to accepting the whole of me.

I find it so funny that it took being a grown person with kids before I learned to honor myself. Why was this not taught in school? Why weren't parents teaching this? Where had the system gone wrong?

I can hear the teachers now, " Honoring yourself? What about all those poor children who don't have time to honor themselves?" Everything in my school was about giving and more giving. More misguided pollution.

Our universe is regulated by a number of spiritual laws or principles. One of these is that the Universe operates through a dynamic energy flow where output and input are equal. This law is known as the *law of giving and receiving.*

If we give, yet block ourselves from receiving, we break the flow of what naturally should be an equal exchange of energy. For instance, if I am always giving of my time and resources and someone offers to help me or give back to me and I decline the offer while continuing to offer my time and resources, I soon feel drained of energy and incapable of giving. I likely become resentful and feel I have no more of myself to give because I have broken the flow of giving and receiving.

When we honor ourselves and treat ourselves sacredly, we naturally begin to understand this universal law. There is an old African saying, "You cannot ask a naked man for a shirt." When we honor ourselves, we don't allow ourselves to become naked or energetically empty. And the sacredness allows us to bring the best into our living and being. We take the time to receive support and attention to refill our energy reserves so we can bring more goodness to everything we do and to the world. Our souls dance when we are creating and expanding with love!

I feel that if we all honored ourselves, we would have a world of happier and more accepting and calm people.

SKILLS FOR YOUR JOURNEY

Here are exercises you can do to practice honoring yourself and treating yourself as a sacred being.

- **Honor yourself.** Begin by making a list of different areas of your life and how they affect you in body, mind, and spirit. Once you have written your list, it will be time to act on what you have listed.

  If you decide to begin with honoring your body, then, each day, add one more action from your list to your daily routine. As you honor yourself, remember to add sacredness to clear your mind, body, and spirit. For example: On Monday, I start to observe what I am feeding my body. I ask: *Is it good for me? Is the food I am choosing nourishing? Is it what my body really wants or is it just a habit? Am I eating on the run?* Before I eat something, I ask myself, *What does this food offer me?* Then, I eat with full focus on the food and experience how much it nourishes and fills me.

  On Tuesday, I have a choice. I can choose to do more of what my body already showed me it wants and needs to be healthy and feel good. Each day of that week, I may choose to work on one or two of the same listed assessments or different ones.

  By the time that you reach the end of your list of assessments of what makes your body feel healthy and good, you will be honoring your body and probably feeling much healthier.

  Next, you could begin adding another category, maybe from honoring your mind to your daily assessments. Or ways to honor your soul . . . and carry on from there. It is important to go slow, add the sacredness and evolve at your own pace. This may be the most self-awakening segment in the book. Enjoy!

Of course, this description of how to self-assess what your body, mind, and soul want is just a suggestion. For the most benefits, work through your list at your own speed. If you really focus on incorporating the questions on this list into your everyday life, you will soon discover a huge difference in your perspective of your life and yourself.

The most wonderful aspect of this revealing skill is that you learn about your genuine characteristics and how you live the best . About what makes you who you are. Once you know these things, you won't be influenced by other people's habits or feel pulled to do what society deems correct. Each of us is special and has our own beauty. Making and implementing your list will help you discover and feel alive in that beauty.

Body Assessments
What am I feeding my body?
How much water do I consume?
Am I exercising and stretching?
How much and how well am I sleeping?
With what kind of background noises do I surround myself?
How much time do I allow myself to "just be"?
How much time do I spend in nature?
Do I dress in ways that I like?
Am I hanging around people I enjoy?

Am I spending time with people I dislike?

Am I being my genuine self in everything I do?

Mind Assessments

What do I feed my mind?

Do I learn something new every day?

Am I conscious and in the present? How much of the time?

Do I allow myself time to daydream and visualize?

Am I living more from the critical side of my mind?

Am I meditating every day?

Am I centered 90 percent of the time?

Do I feel sufficiently stimulated (or overstimulated)?

Am I increasing my ability to focus?

Do I let random thoughts fill my head?

Soul Assessments

Am I nourishing my soul every day? How?

How often do I open myself to hearing my soul?

What am I listening to (conversations, music, and so on)? Does what I hear bring me closer to my soul or farther away?

How much time do I spend in my sacred space growing?

Do I honor the sacredness of life?

Do I open myself to the wonder and curiosity of life? To Spirit?

Do I allow myself to see beauty in others and in myself?

How often do I dance, feel free, alive?

- **Open yourself to giving.** Now that you are filling yourself and feeding your body, mind, and spirit, you can begin to give in a way that isn't from "I have to . . ." or to please other people. Now you are giving because you want to give.

  Importantly, giving without conditions is a way to open yourself to receiving. Receiving comes when we give from the heart—without wanting something in return. When we give in this way, God/the Universe showers us with gifts we may never have previously imagined. We always receive more than we give.

  If you have difficulty receiving, this is the time to ask yourself, *Why?* Open yourself to the sacred experience of receiving. Even create an atmosphere of asking for help and graciously, sacredly receiving it.

  By opening yourself to true giving and receiving, you are living the law of receiving, and joy and wonder will fill your life. This is an amazing way to honor yourself and others at the same time.

Chapter 5

Hearing Your Soul

*Hello, Soul. Lead me through each step I need to take
to know you better and help me create a life
which pleases my heart.*

As my connection with my soul deepened, I felt an urge to find out more about it. I was determined to live in complete connection to my divine inner essence.

My amazement with how I grew as an individual by simply honoring my body, mind, and spirit prompted many new questions to arise in my mind. *Why did my soul/I want to come here? What was I born to learn? Is there a purpose?* And, *Who is Alena's soul?*

I met with a friend, who is a shaman, for coffee to discuss how to really talk to my soul. He told me to practice two things: 1. Open myself to wonder and rhythm—to dance, poetry, and life; and 2: Learn everything I could about the soul. To this day, I still thank him for not simply telling me about the soul but instead suggesting that I do my own research to discover and learn. The journey of learning was fun and personal.

That very day, I began to activate my senses. My urge was to connect to the rhythm of life and nature, so I took a walk in a nature preserve by my house. It was winter and the conditions were perfect—not overly cold, just a light breeze, beautiful sun, and everything covered in white snow.

Nature has always been where I am able to form my strongest connection to my soul, which craves connection, cohesiveness, and freedom. My soul was ecstatic at this new adventure. I stood quietly by the frozen pond in the woods, closed my eyes, and tried to hear the rhythm. Was there a rhythm to nature and life like my shaman friend told me? I was about to find out.

First, I concentrated on my own breath. As I listened to my own personal rhythm of breathing in and out, the environment came alive. I heard a nuthatch peck the wood of the tree in his own repeated pattern. A breeze rustled the leaves of the tree, softly creating syncopation to the pecking. A cardinal began to sing, bringing its special melody. Between each phrase of its voice, I could hear the ice on the pond creaking as it condensed. The final piece that made the music of the woods come together was the far-off call of a coyote. The sounds of the scene were like a symphony.

I continued to listen for a little while, allowing myself to become part of the community of patterns and syncopation. My body actually began to move to this very calm rhythm.

Could this be what my friend was speaking of—is this the rhythm of life? I wondered.

As I allowed myself to become more integrated with my surroundings, I started to sense a bigger rhythm underlining all the activity. It is actually hard to explain. I can only say that it felt like I was sensing the heartbeat of all life including the life of the earth, stars, and sky above.

I was astounded. It was truly so calming and consistent. Everything seemed to be breathing to the same rhythm—a universal rhythm. I felt my heart match the calm, consistent beat. This rhythm is the reason shamans use a steady drumbeat to transcend ordinary reality during ceremonies—they are bringing forth the universal rhythm so they can transcend and open the veil of life. This was a new awakening for me.

This universal rhythm of all life is a sign of our oneness. Any time I open to this rhythm, my body slows into it. Every part of me vibrates with it. Now that I am aware of it, never again do I ever have to do anything except connect to this rhythm to connect to life and to my soul.

From that point on, nature opened to me. It was as if it knew I had heard and felt the rhythm. One time, I traveled to Los Angeles, California, to speak at an event. After the event, I drove up to Lake Arrowhead in the San Bernardino Mountains to meet someone who wanted to do an event with me. When I arrived, I found myself exhausted. I had helped people continually for three days while partaking in the event in LA and now I just wanted to renew my energy. I decided to get up early the next morning to take a hike and spend the morning with the natural world and connecting to my soul.

The next morning, I found a trail to hike at a nature preserve close to where I was staying and began my hike. The warm sun brought a balance to the chill in the morning air. The contrast of these sensations felt good as I hiked up the little mountain and took in the outstanding views on the path. At the top of the mountain, there were three sequoia trees nestled together with a little space between them that seemed like a perfect spot for meditation. So, I sat down among these statuesque beings, thanked them for allowing me to be with them, and began to meditate totally in sync with the rhythm of all life.

When I opened my eyes, there were two little sparrows standing in front of me. I said hello and thanked them for having been with me during my meditation. As I got up, they did not move, so I told them, "It is time for me to walk down the mountain. You may join me if you like." And they did! They joined me. This cute pair of birds hopped in front of me down the side of this magical mountain.

As the three of us walked together, we came upon a big, flat rock lying in the sun. I could not resist. I lay down on that big rock to enjoy the sunshine and soon fell asleep. When I awoke, I looked down from my rock to find not only my two friendly birds, but also a fox and some squirrels and rabbits. Little friendly animals were all playing around me and my rock.

This incident epitomizes just one of the incredible way's nature has opened itself to me ever since I first felt the universal rhythm and understood its patterns and syncopations. Nature is amazing and magical!

The more fully I participated in the flow and rhythm of the world around me, the more it connected with me. And when I allowed myself to release into this rhythm, my soul came alive. I would carry on full conversations or receive ideas or concepts as my body moved with the slow, rhythmic beat that bonds the entire universe. My soul began contacting me more frequently each day through words, feelings, and how I saw my world—in fact, it was as if this rhythm had activated something inside me that open my ability to hear my soul.

To encourage this communication with my soul I again entered nature. This time in the early morning sitting amidst the trees in my own backyard. I brought out my cup of tea and made myself comfortable in what I felt was the most magical part of my yard. Why was it magical? There was this strong feeling among all the trees. Walking on the stone path I could see how one tree had fallen leaning on another tree creating a feeling of a portal. And if you veered towards that portal the tree turned into a feeling of woods. I felt like everything communicated with each other, everything belonged, and I was the visitor. I kept walking on this veered off path and came to the gorge. Immediately my whole spiritual self-felt as if it had been transported to another time and place. Something very magical about the gorge. Every time I look at it. I am hypnotized.

As always I felt an immense feeling of awe and wonder. It is here that I sat down with my cup of tea and began to ask my soul, "How may I serve?" The first few times I asked, I heard nothing. Then one morning as I sat in my very special spot, eyes closed feeling the massiveness of our world and universe, I heard a soft, gentle voice reply, "Have fun today!"

At first, I was stunned. *Did I just answer myself? Is this real?*

My soul had answered me, and I heard it! How soothing and gentle it sounded. I felt a sense of all-knowingness and calm because I was connecting to the essence of my whole being, my inner divinity.

"How are you?" I asked.

"I am you and we are at peace," the soft voice replied.

"How may I serve the world today?"

"Open yourself completely to your wonderment and curiosity. This will bring you closer to God/the Universe—our Source."

A sureness filled my being. I felt grounded and whole and the tense urgency in my stomach and shoulders relaxed. It was as if my whole body and mind had evolved to a place of love and completeness.

Hearing my soul speak back to me created a sense of aliveness in me. I found myself wanting to connect to everything—the trees, the ground, the people. I wanted to see them through the eyes of my soul!

This was the beginning of my vision of a whole new world.

What Is Soul?

Growing up in the Catholic religion, I heard a lot about the "born sin" of our souls, or "original sin," but I was never taught what the soul was. I just assumed it was the spiritual side of us.

Once I started to help souls go into the light after death, I gained an understanding that the soul comes from God, the Beloved. Or the Universe if you prefer that language. Because of this experience and meditations on my soul, I feel the soul is our being in the light.

I have worked with spiritual practices from many other religions, including indigenous wisdom traditions, as an adult. Some people believe that humankind comes from the stars. I do not know if this is the case or not; however, it is a great way to describe our souls. Our souls are parts of one massive field of energy. And although we are small parts of something vast, the unique soul of each human on earth belongs to the vastness of the whole.

The soul is an energetic part of us that chooses to come to Earth and inhabit or connect with a body and experience a personal plan to learn and grow so that it can evolve. And this personal evolution causes the mass universe of light to evolve. As each of us awakens and gains greater understanding, we, as souls, evolve the entire universe.

Now, there are many different beliefs about what the soul is and its reason for being. My personal belief stems from my experiences with the lost souls of dead people that come to me, and from the gifts of my own soul, which I receive during meditation.

After I began my journey to awaken to the presence and live by my soul, I was gifted with many new opportunities to experience the light and gain more perspective on the nature of the human soul.

One meditation, which wasn't even a real meditation, spontaneously occurred when I was exhausted and had flopped myself down on my bed. I allowed every muscle in my body to relax. As I told my Beloved how extremely tired I was, I suddenly felt an incredible, overwhelming sensation of unconditional love wash over me and fill my heart with peace along with such immense joy that it me made giggle. And then it was gone. My Beloved God had allowed me to feel the light. For some reason, I was supposed to see what it was like to be "home," by which I mean "unified with our incredible Universe."

Another time, I had a remarkable vision. I was visiting my favorite, sparkling waterfall when a form of light approached and melded into me.

I want to be clear on this. The form of light did not enter my body. It melded to my soul, which is not physical. I was informed, as this was occurring, that the spirit of the Beloved is part of all our souls, and we are parts of it. We are melded and exist in unity. What this means is that, as we open to our souls, we can recognize our full unity with the Beloved.

Now to be clear, this is my own realization, not that of a religion or other belief system. It is from my own experience and growth resulting from connection with my soul. I also want to share that although I am writing about this discovery in one chapter, it has taken me time to develop this understanding of the soul. It was as if opening the door to the universal rhythm of life made it possible for my meditations, my visions, and communication with my soul to occur; however, these events did not all occur at once. Experience and teachers filled my world whenever it was time for me to learn. Sometimes I felt it was time for me to learn like when I decided it was time to hear from my soul. Remember what I said earlier in this chapter about how it took me a few times asking, *Are you there, Soul? to hear* its soft loving voice. Each time I asked, I had to practice being more open to receiving my soul and to let go of the critical mind. When it was time for me to hear the soul was when I was ready to receive it.

This is very important for us because we are so used to getting things right away and even told to deliver our work or services immediately. There is a level of patience when we are growing and learning to hear and live by our soul. So, relax and enjoy the process, which is a lesson in itself.

How My Soul Grew in My Life

By listening to the soft voice of my soul, I have come to realize that our souls are all about creating, expanding, and loving. How I experienced this myself was that ideas would fill my mind, followed by overwhelming happiness when something I created or wanted to happen became part of my reality.

After a while, instead of asking my soul, "How may I serve?" Every morning, I said, "What would be fun today?" The answer would come into my ear and mind immediately. I'd get answers like "Dance" or "Invite a friend to the movies." As every day brought something new, I woke with such excitement, anticipating it would be fun.

Until I connected with my soul on a conscious level, I always thought that living with my soul would be serious; I imagined that I would always be meditating and speaking in high and lofty tones. However, it is quite different. It is magical.

Being guided by my soul means getting guidance from something all-knowing, which means that everything just flows easier. My life today really feels like magic. I feel lighter, happier, more content, and freer to experience and enjoy the world I am creating.

One day, I awoke with an incredible urge to go to a coffee shop and journal. *Really?* I hadn't journaled since I kept a diary in high school. *Journal?* However, I trusted what I felt and heard. So, I dropped the kids off at school and went notepad in hand, to a coffee shop and began writing. To my surprise, I kept writing and writing for a full hour. *Wow!* This was new to me. I had never enjoyed writing this much before. The next day, I was back at the coffee shop writing up a storm again.

This went on for three months. Before I knew it, I had a book, my very first, *You Can't Escape from a Prison If You Don't Know You're in One!* which was published six years ago.

From that moment on, people started to fill my life for the sole purpose of getting that book out into the world. It truly was magical. When I was typing my journal into my laptop at the coffee shop, I found myself arguing with the computer. A man from the other end of the table I was sitting at started to laugh, and I couldn't help smiling at him . He asked, "Are you an author?"

Was I ready to say I was an author? That was a big step. I heard the soft voice say, "You did write the book." So, I said to the man, "Yes, and this is my first book." He laughed again and told me that he was a published author and would love to help me.

That, my friend, is the magic of not only my soul but of God/the Universe.

The magic was back in my life! *Hallelujah!*

In truth, there is magic all around us. Our souls try to communicate with us about the magic of the Universe, especially its creative power. When I opened myself to the rhythm of life and the universal rhythm, I opened myself to a powerful understanding of oneness.

I also gained the understanding that if I am one with everything then everything is me. I am to allow myself to see everything through this connection: through the eyes of my soul.

When we were young, we were open to this understanding and flow of the Universe. We were familiar with a sense of newness and discovery because we ourselves were always creating through our imagination as we were playing. We were filled with wonder and fascination for the movement of the entire natural world.

When I was five, my family moved from Arizona to Vermont and I saw my first snow. I was astounded; it was like magic. I simply could not get enough of this fluffy white stuff. It was like the clouds were coming down to us. At every possible moment that winter, I was outside sledding, building snow people, or more likely, throwing snowballs—my new discovery.

Why can't we be filled with this fearless feeling of wonder, discovery, and exploring? Why must we become so serious, critical, and self-important? We take everything as if our lives depend on it? We put ourselves through the absolute worstsituations because we feel that we must. We have fallen victim to the belief that if something we want to achieve or possess isn't hard to do or get then it's not worth it.

Well, I have news for you. Life is not supposed to be hard. It is supposed to be a time for us to experience the contrasts of the light that exist in the world, and then deliberately unify with the light. It truly is this simple. Once we learn the lessons from these contrasts, we evolve spiritually. An example of this would be if I suffered a betrayal from a lover or friend. Being betrayed is a contrast to the unconditional love of the Universe. Feeling the sadness and anger and even an inability to trust anyone for a period may be a part of the experience. Once I had felt those things, I would have the option to accept what it is, learn a higher lesson from it, and let it go. Or I could hang on to the hurt feelings, swear never to trust again, and wear my pain as a badge of being a survivor.

If I take the first option, I am experiencing the contrast, learning from it, and moving forward free. And because I let go of my own hurt and anger, I can open myself to a higher lesson that evolves my soul and sets me free from the experience here on earth.

How we choose to experience these contrasts is up to us. We are responsible for the journey we chose or how we want to evolve. It is either the short and easier road of the soul or the harder and longer road of realization.

So, if we connect with our souls and unify with the Universe will the rest of our lives be effortless? The answer is a resounding NO! Remember, we are here to experience the contrasts between the light (heaven) and what happens in our lives. That means we are here to discover the opposite of unconditional love, joy, and peace.

We are also here to experience the creation process—to learn how to manifest. This process is what causes us to evolve spiritually. It is the main reason we choose to exist on this plane of existence.

What living in unity with our souls allows us to do is to see the world through a higher version of what is. Meaning, we see the situations we're in and the challenges we face from a higher perspective. Metaphorically, we are above the trees instead of inside the forest. This allows us to access universal answers and guidance that alleviates the worry, anger, questioning, and angst so many of us suffer while not connected to our souls. Any time we doubt and worry, it is a sure sign that we are connected to our critical monkey minds or egos.

I guess it comes down to one question: How do you want to walk this journey of life: Do you want to take the road of the critical mind or the road of the soul?

Only you can answer this question—and you answer it through your decisions of how you live today, tomorrow, and the next day and the day after that.

We all come to a point where we fully connect with our souls and the universe. Many people connect only when they die. Speaking for myself, I chose to have that full, beautiful, and magical connection NOW while I am alive. What about you?

Yes, we are connected to the whole world. Whenever we decide to open to the magic of spirit, a magical reality will open to us—*true* reality. We just need to learn to believe again.

Expressing gratitude and saying hello to the gifts of your soul are the first couple of steps in the journey of opening your soul to you.

SKILLS FOR YOUR JOURNEY

It is time to learn a powerful skill that will help you open to wonder and awe.

- **Establish a gratitude practice.** The very best way to open up to your soul is with gratitude. I realize that gratitude rituals are talked about a lot; however, some rituals do not bring us to the state of wonder that is ideal. I'm going to teach you a way that does!

  Before you begin your gratitude practice, pick out a nice writing notebook—perhaps a fancy one with a fabric or leather covering. Why is it so special? Because your gratitude time will be special and treating it as such will help you to be consistent in practicing this habit going forward. Also, designate a time and a place of comfort/sacred space for the morning and nighttime to practice expressing gratitude.

  Do the following things at every session:

  1. Once you are settled and comfortable, write a phrase you like on top of the page to begin. A good friend of mine likes to write: "So happy and grateful now that . . ." (The ellipsis leaves room for what comes in Step 2.) My own preference is: "Thank you! Thank you!"

  2. After you have your title, make a list of things you are grateful for in your life. As you write the list, it is of utmost importance to *feel* gratefulness for these things. Use your imagination to invoke emotions. An example would be how when I write

about my big, red dog, I imagine the feeling of him licking my face or jumping up onto the bed beside me. It brings a big smile to my face as I do.

Feeling is the most important part of the gratitude session. Feeling raises our mood to an amazing state. Also, it helps our bodies and minds send out wonderful frequencies to the Universe, vibes that are energetically saying, "Thank you so much, I am so happy!" The Universe then responds by giving us more things to be happy about.

3. After you finish your list of gratitude, ask God/the Universe, "How may I serve?" or "Do you have a message for me for the day?" Then, allow yourself to relax, close your eyes, and listen peacefully. Sometimes you will hear or see something in your mind and sometimes it is just a peaceful moment.

4. When you are ready, send loving light to three people or situations that are bothering you. Yes, you read this suggestion correctly! Sending loving light and seeing it in your mind's eye wrapping around and loving the person or situation will help those people and situations greatly.

Gratefulness is how you can begin the process of opening yourself to rhythm whether that is music, nature and then take the leap to the universal rhythm or the rhythm of life. Remember this is slow and only as fun as you make it. I found that if I strived to hear the rhythm of the universe, then I would definitely not hear it. It happens when we have created the environment to open all ourselves to it like I did in the park on that cold winter morning I told you about earlier in the chapter.

- **Take time to sit in a place that offers you peace and a bit of awe**. Relax and open to the space allowing your mind to come to the present moment. This would be a great place to even do your gratitude to help you come into the present in the best vibration.

Once you are calm and open, ask your soul, "Are you there, Soul?" or "How may I serve the world in the best way?" It may take a few times; however, do not get discouraged. It is all about becoming ready to receive. The more you come to this place, the more open and in the presence of the space, the more you will become ready to hear that soft, loving, and powerful voice of your soul.

Enjoy the environment you are creating and experiencing around you. The rhythm of the Universe will appear when you are truly open to it. It usually comes when you least expect it. Enjoy the process of opening.

Chapter 6

What Stops Us from True Connection?

The only thing that stops us from feeling the richness and depth of our true connection to God/the Universe is us.

When I sat in the forest clearing and momentarily succumbed to my despair about my divorce, the response from the natural world blew my mind. It had been the worst day of my life. For the first time in my life, I was at a loss at how to proceed. The divorce and the damage it was doing to my family felt like too much for me to handle. How was I going to protect my boys and keep our family strong? How was I going to remain strong as this divorce seemed to become harder and harder?

I got into my car and drove. My car is my refuge when I feel I need to think or just let go. I put on music and let the car take me. This time I ended up in an adjacent town. I knew the town because I had once lived and worked there. What was new to me was the road I found myself on. Up ahead, I saw a stone fence. This intrigued me because I absolutely love stone fences. Once I reached the fence, I saw it traveled up a hill. My car and I followed the fence up to an old monastery whose grounds were filled with old, majestic-looking trees.

I parked the car and walked over to a clearing. I collapsed into a seated position on the ground. I was surrendering my life to this wonderful place. Every part of me was tired and I needed relief. Closing my eyes, I let all thoughts leave my mind. It was then that I felt a light breeze kiss my check and a very odd sensation: the majestic trees surrounding the clearing were leaning in towards me.

Keeping my eyes closed, I allowed my shoulders to drop and asked for wisdom. It was then I heard a "caw" above me. I opened my eyes to see a red-tailed hawk circling me and cawing. Something caught my eye on the ground. I looked to see hundreds of insects circling me in the same direction as the hawk. No insect touched me. *Is all this really happening to me? Did the Universe open to me just to show me how we are all one—in total connection? Did I really feel the trees leaning towards me and did I truly see the insects and the hawk circling me, or was it just my imagination?*

I then realized I was critically analyzing a gift from the Universe and stopped myself. No, I was not going to allow this to happen! I would not listen to my reasoning mind deconstruct the gift the Universe gave me. I sensed that this gift was meant to change my whole belief system about my individual connection to the Earth and the rest of the cosmos.

Finally, I released my fear and all the heaviness from my shoulders, head, arms, and body. Allowing myself to cry with relief, I finally understood. I was not alone! I was part of the whole universe and it was part of me. I understood that it hears me and feels what I feel because we are one.

In retrospect, it really is no wonder that my belief system and critical mind was trying to diminish this beautiful experience. It went against everything I grew up being taught to believe by my parents, teachers, church, and friends. My whole reality was changing, and my critical mind was in a panic.

I understood that my mind wanted me to be safe—but I didn't like how it was going about the task. I didn't want to be trapped in my comfort zone. I didn't want to allow it to keep me from connecting to the Divine. The question I kept coming back to was this: *Am I to believe what I felt and saw, as I experienced it, or instead what my mind says it has to be?*

I knew that I wanted to have a full magical connection to my divine inner self, my soul. Out in the woods that day, I finally began to understand that the only things holding me back from this powerful connection were my beliefs: the labels and criticisms that I would hear over and over in my head. A critical voice in my mind held me back in various situations and, as a result, I was leading a life that wasn't serving me well anymore.

For years, I had been trying to ignore my negative thoughts, to pretend they were not there. It did not work.

Long-held beliefs derived from our past experiences can be strong. Mine would sabotage any progress I tried to achieve. They altered my perception in a way that kept opportunities at bay. Recently, I had noticed that whenever I had a vivid spiritual experience, I would hear dismissive thoughts in my head about it, such as, *That is too easy. It can't be real. It's a trick.* Or worse, that critical voice would say, *You really think all of nature gathered around you? Who are you to have such gifts?* Our beliefs can be cruel.

Beliefs can be so strong sometimes that they can keep us from trying new things, venturing out of areas we know, and consciously connecting with our souls and God/the Universe. I loved what happened at the monastery, however, I felt like I had to justify the magical moment and make it whatever my old beliefs wanted it to be.

It can take a while to learn to discern between the sound of your soul speaking to you and the sound of your critical mind speaking to you and trying to reinforce your old beliefs. But it is important to learn to do so because, as Albert Einstein has been attributed as saying, "We cannot solve our problems with the same thinking we used when we created them."

This is logical, isn't it? If we want to evolve as people, don't we need to open ourselves to new opportunities in which we can learn? Sadly, too many of us are so stuck in doing what we were told to do and thinking what we were told to think that we can't see the possibilities in anything different and new.

I decided to put my critical mind and its so-called beliefs of what happened to me that miraculous day as I sat in a clearing at a beautiful, old stone monastery to the test. From that day forward, I made a point to fully accept how I felt, what I saw, and what I knew deep inside. And this opened the door for me to look at my whole belief system regarding ideas of heaven, My Beloved God's omnipresence, and my part in all of it. In opening myself to this new experience, I opened my mind to a bigger, more loving, and more powerful connection to everything that is than I had ever thought was possible.

Sure, many old beliefs were shattered. But it was time. A whole new world was beginning to show itself to me, and I was ready to take a journey to explore it.

Gradually, I found that I could distinguish the voice of my soul from other voices in my head. I loved checking in with it at random moments of the day. While driving, I would ask, "Are you with me, Soul?" and in reply I would hear, "Of course, Alena. I am here."

My soul was always whispering its guidance in my ear, and I felt a deep contentment that all in life was and would continue to be fine. This gave me the courage to step out of my comfort zone and have new experiences.

Of course, my critical ego mind would pronounce loudly that each was not a good idea. But instead of only listening to all the limitations it was pointing out I would trick my critical mind into submission by using one simple phrase: "How fun it would be to learn more about . . ." This phrase felt non-threatening to my critical mind—it knew that fun was not dangerous! It was okay for me just to see whatever there was to see.

A major benefit of silencing the inner critic was that it allowed me to hear my soul, which was always ready to dance with opportunity. Each time I allowed myself to open to a new experience, I learned more and more of the truth that was meant for me.

The voice of my critical ego mind became softer as I became more connected to my soul. The best part of the transformation I was undergoing was when magic began to appear in my life everywhere and every day.

Bye-Bye, Critical Mind

Tricking the critical mind only works for so long because of how smart it is. However, there are ways to permanently weaken an old belief system that plagues our evolution. One great way to begin is with the method we used to start the process: by sacredly honoring ourselves and returning to the soulful "I." It is in honoring ourselves that we begin to gain respect for and trust in our ability to connect with our souls. If we allow it, we can open our minds to other possibilities and ways of being.

Happiness and clarity of mind is a natural result of honoring our feelings, ideas, and desire for growth. If we allow our feelings to be as they are, new possibilities and possible ways of being emerge. Unfortunately, many find it difficult to honor themselves. The critical mind has to weaken the major belief we as a society have been taught. That belief is that honoring selfish. I too, had a bit of guilt every time I started to take time for myself or change habits that benefited me. And because guilt is not something I like to feel, I found ways to conquer it so I could honor myself fully.

Earlier in my journey of growth, I had learned the power of affirmations and emotion to help change the critical mind's old beliefs. An affirmation is a statement or phrase we want to believe that either counteracts an old belief we'd like to clear from our mental programming or describes a version of reality we'd like to live.

When I wanted to be an international bestseller, I wrote out an affirmation stating, "I am an international bestseller. My book will be helping thousands and my career will be launched." Now that I had the affirmation, I had to find the best way to use it so that my critical mind would accept it easily. I also wanted the Universe/God to hear my heartfelt desire.

To do this, I had to use my affirmation and emotions to change any old belief that I wasn't an author or that being an international bestseller was too difficult. I had to send a clear message to the Universe that I was ready.

I utilized the affirmation in a few ways. First, I would say my affirmation in the mirror both morning and night. I would look myself in the eye and repeat it until I believed it.

Second, before each meal of the day, I would write out my affirmation twenty-five times.

I would also repeat the affirmation aloud multiple times a day to make it real for my critical mind.

But my favorite way was when I made a recording of my voice repeating it over and over. This recording even had a lively musical accompaniment. And I added inspirational messages to the track to build myself up, like, "I am so proud of you, Alena. Your life has changed. Your business is off and running. Your children are happy and successful."

I would listen to my recording as I put on makeup, drove in the car, and cooked dinner. I loved the recording and music because it raised my mood and made me dance.

Does it sound like I surrounded myself with my chosen belief? Yes, I most certainly did. With each day, my certainty and happiness grew. The more I said and felt the affirmation, the easier it was to go through the process of writing, editing, and sending my manuscript to the publisher and getting the final product on the shelves. I increasingly believed I truly was an international bestselling author.

On the day of my book launch, I received a call. By noon I was, indeed, an international bestselling author.

That is the power of affirmations and belief.

I also used an affirmation when I wanted to connect to my soul. This new affirmation really was more of a mantra I heard from my soul one time: "Spirit is Love and Love is Spirit." Now, I did not create a recording, as it wasn't that type of desire. I already felt this yearning deep inside me. This affirmation or mantra quieted any critic in me when I said it. It opened my mind to my heart, which then led me to feel love and align with my soul. Once that connection was established, I began to see through the eyes of my soul and to process my perceptions with wonder and in a childlike, accepting way.

When did I use a new affirmation? Any time I felt a critical, old belief coming on, I would say it with purpose and passion. It was working well.

Taoist Meditation

A powerful way to disperse mental and emotional blocks comes from Taoism. Remember, *Tao* means "the Way." Taoism is a way of living, thinking, and aligning with the Beloved/the Divine Universe. One Taoist meditation helps us to rid ourselves from blocks caused by our old beliefs.

Here is how to do it. Start by getting comfortable and relaxing in a way that works for you. Then take three cleansing breaths. Begin by breathing in all goodness and spirit, filling your abdomen and feeling renewed as you do. As you breathe out, allow all that does not serve you to leave your body.

Then, once you are relaxed, feeling heavy, and sinking in your chair or floor, visualize a pure white light above your head. Allow this light to enter the crown of your head. See it making its way ever so slowly down through your body, looking for anything that is blocking its path. Any time the flow of the light stops, you have found a block of old beliefs or the residue of experiences that is holding you back.

When the light reaches a block, take time to speak with the block. Get curious. What is the block? What is its story? Once you receive an answer, you may then choose either to keep the block or to disperse it and give it back to the Universe.

I find I feel ten times freer when I do this powerful meditation. To make sure that block doesn't come back, I use an affirmation or fill my mind with videos, books, or people confirming the belief I want to have in my whole self.

The more I grow on my journey to connect with my soul, I know and feel that the Universe and God are waiting for me.

I am always supposed to connect to understand and accept my true self and connect to even a higher truth.

We are supposed to wake up, and we all eventually do. However, it is much more fun and rewarding to wake up now while we have time to live with the magic in this world. And all it takes is opening to it! Given that this could not be any simpler, why are there still about 95 percent of our population who still allow the beliefs imposed on them by others stand in their way? That's what I wonder.

I love hearing my soul and how my eyes are beginning to open to the signs and magic of the Universe. But it still didn't always feel like I had heard or felt my soul's complete message. Sometimes I wonder if I had heard wrong or misinterpreted the message. How can this be? I am open, so what is going on?

I always have wanted to have a full connection—to hear everything my soul has to say to me clearly and to have a complete conversation with it. But to be truthful, until very recently I have felt there was still something screwing my interpretation of what I heard from soul. Actually, my soul was eager to be in full communication. The miscommunication was a problem on my end. What was screwing this up?

That is when a teacher appeared and moved me forward in my journey!

SKILLS FOR YOUR JOURNEY

Now, it's your turn again to practice skills to connect with your soul. Here are three ideas.

- **Declare a day of choice.** This is a day when you can choose who you want to be and what you want to think. It is also a day without blame, defending, or judging yourself and others. Simply observe yourself as you go about your activities and when you see yourself say, do, or even think something you don't want to say, do, or think, then stop and proclaim, "Redo."

  Here's an example of how this will work. Let's say you are walking down the street and see someone dressed in bright colors, like a clown. The first thought in your head is something judgmental about the clothing: *That guy looks ridiculous!* or *Those bright colors are ugly.* Once you notice that you have thought the thought, stop and say, "Redo." Then make a neutral observation, like: *That guy is wearing bright clothing, Wow, the blue looks really nice on him.*

  Do this without punishing yourself for the original thought or action. Just observe and change whatever thoughts or actions you would like to change. This technique can work in any situation and with any critical thought.

  If you make every day a day of choice, soon you won't even have to say, "Redo," because your choices and thought processes will be different than they once were.

- **Create an affirmation that promotes the achievement of your goals.** Is there something that you dream of accomplishing in your life? It can be anything—maybe it is simply connecting to your soul. Awesome! Whatever it may be, using an affirmation can be a powerful way to focus your intention and help you attain this goal. The trick is to generate a strong positive feeling about your goal when you say or hear the affirmation. Feel it in your body!

If you wanted to open more to hearing the voice of your soul, you might say the affirmation "I am open to listening to guidance from my soul." As you say this affirmation, in your mind visualize what it would be like to hear the voice of your soul and to feel connection. Allow happiness, excitement, and peace to fill your whole being.

You could record the same affirmation, like I did when I was writing my first book, so you could play it back whenever you want. You could listen to it everywhere you go. You could also sing it like a song and dance with joy as you do to show the Universe how happy this makes you feel. It is the feeling of joy and excitement that will get your soul involved in any project you do. As positive feelings grow, new beliefs will form in your mind, which will help you to change your old beliefs with ease. Without feeling and affirmations, it is much harder to believe that a goal is achievable.

Here is another affirmation for you. Try saying: "I am open to receiving all abundance, happiness, and connection to my soul and bring them into my everyday life."

- **From time to time, ask, "Are you there, Soul?"** Maybe you will hear a response and maybe you won't. The purpose of this action is to open a door inside yourself that makes you available to hearing or seeing spiritual messages. Some people hear their guidance—usually very auditory people. Others see colors or images in their mind's eyes. Still others may smell or feel their souls. Everyone is wired differently and there is no wrong or right to this.

In my opinion, it is time that we open ourselves to these different ways and see how our own inner divine comes to us.

Chapter 7
Good-Bye Baggage

Birds let go of whatever holds them from flying.
Planes limit the amount of luggage so that they can fly.
Why do we want to carry all our baggage and fly so low?

Changing my beliefs about myself and my capabilities and opening myself to a world of imagination, trust, and my soul was creating greater ease and synchronicity in my life. But something was still holding me back, as if with chains from an invisible source. *What is this?* I wondered. I thought I had done the work necessary to free myself when I improved my beliefs. But these "chains" felt more like heavy energy in my heart.

Through meditation, I began to inquire about the source of the heaviness. I found anger, the pain of betrayal, and sadness. Even though I had done inner work to change my beliefs about the people and situations associated with these feelings, I still held a feeling of anger for my mom and priest for not believing me when I told them of my spiritual gifts as a child and for saying that using them would be evil.

As I delved deeper into the story of my anger, I found that although I had forgiven my mom and the priest, I was holding the energy of the anger inside the belief it had caused me to form. That long standing belief—which I had been holding on to for years—was that I could not tell anyone about my spirituality or my gifts because they would find me strange or even evil.

Could these stored emotions and the lessons they created be holding me back from fully immersing myself in the magic of the world? That's what I wanted—no, needed—to know.

Asking *How can I heal these strong emotions and their lessons? How can I release the chains on my heart?* initiated the next leg of my journey, which involved forgiving both others and me.

Forgiving Others

I began my search. *Wow, there are so many programs, books, and teachings on forgiveness,* I thought. *There must be many people just like me trying to learn.* All the programs offered interesting ways to forgive; however, two specific styles helped me the most. Although these two methods were similar, each offered something special. I combined them to develop a style of forgiveness that was all my own.

Sometimes that can happen. We are all slightly different in our way of accepting new ideas or ways of being. One shoe does not fit all, so we must take the time to try out new things, then take the parts that work best for us. I guess being really good at helping people adapt various techniques to meet their needs is what led me to become a spiritual mentor. The methods I have drawn together come from science, different religious traditions, a variety of healing modalities, and my personal life experience.

The first method of forgiveness I embraced came from my shaman friend, who told me that my whole spiritual journey was my way of working through my chakra system.

Chakras are energy portals that are our connections between the physical world and the Universe, my shaman friend told me. The ancient founders of the chakra philosophy were tantric philosophers from India. They believed that spiritual and physical life are the same thing—not separate. They realized that the spiritual and physical dance together to form a perfect whole. When we live from this understanding, it truly is like having heaven on earth.

Our spiritual energy surrounds our physical bodies along with being within us. This is why we can see and even photograph our spiritual energy field with a special camera. Each chakra forms its own circle of energy and is located at a certain place within the whole spiritual sphere surrounding us. These circles of energy line up directly with corresponding areas in our physical bodies, forming a line going up from the perineum near our tailbones to above the top of our heads and beyond to the Universe.

Each chakra (energy center) has its own meaning, and through it, we receive spiritual gifts and lessons. We also affect it by how we live our lives or take care of that part of the body. For example, chakra one regulates how we fit into the world and see ourselves. If we feel badly about who we are or have been sexually abused, it will show in the energy of this chakra. When we become conscious of the condition of the chakras and how we affect the chakras with our choices about how we live then we can begin to understand the chakras as the unification of these dimensions of our being. Then life is a magical dance. The dance is us bringing the two together as one in our lives.

The first chakra, which is located at the base of the spine, is the "I" energy center and represents our foundation in this world. Its meaning has to do with the "I" becoming "we." When we enter this world at birth, we are the closest we will ever be to being a pure soul in this lifespan.

As soulful babies, we know what we are here for: to expand, create, and love. We are eager to experience everything—to try new things. We are open to absorbing all that our world has to share. Most importantly, this is the age when we find out where we belong in this big world. Our "I" becoming "we" on earth means finding our community or family. Our connection to the whole universe is made through the family.

Our sense of "we" continues to grow as we discover friends, family, teachers, and colleagues—even through watching TV, reading books and magazines, or surfing the internet on a computer. As our "we" emerges and we build our beliefs about the world and our place in it, the first chakra is impacted.. All our habits, thoughts, values, and fears are formed as we immerse ourselves in the energy of the group we belong to, and we embrace the conformity of the world.

While we are growing up, we absorb both good and not-so-good beliefs. For example, I remember how my dad, while teaching me to swim, said, "You can be anything you want to be as long as you believe in yourself and you go for it." That is a wonderful belief I carry with me to this day. But I also remember forming another belief when my mom was in the hospital having my baby brother. As dad was burning my breakfast, I said to the puppies I was playing with, "Looks like we are on our own from now on." At that moment, I formed a very strong belief in my independence that has been both good and not so good for me. Both beliefs shaped the life I live today as the "we" in society.

The first chakra is associated with the earth because of its stability and strength. However, the earth also can be weakened or strengthened by the experiences it endures. A perfect example is the weakening that occurs because of chemical pollutants getting into the water supply and soil.

The second chakra (aka the *sacral* chakra) is located below the navel and governs the revelation of the self. The energy of this chakra is associated with our personal identity (who we feel we are), an identity we gain while interacting with our families. The consciousness of the sacral chakra is about the flow of our relationships with people and our ability to deal with the dynamics of our lives outside our homes. The condition of this chakra is impacted by how well we make the shift from conforming to the family to forming our own personal world. The sacral chakra is also connected to our sexuality and creation. It helps us to form our desires and it influences the depth of the relationships we create with others.

On an elemental level, the sacral chakra is associated with water because, as we grow older, our concepts of ourselves and our perceptions of the world change. Change and water both flow.

The third chakra is located at the solar plexus. In Sanskrit, an ancient tongue from India, this energy center is called *manipura*, which means "sacred gem." The area of the body where it is located holds our gut instincts and split-second knowing of truth. This pearl of wisdom is the spiritual center for our self-power, well-being, and clarity.

The consciousness of the third chakra is a unification of the consciousness of the first and second chakras. Its element is fire because the energy of this chakra is pulling us between the foundations of chakra one and the changing beliefs we develop as we go about our lives of chakra two. I like to think of chakra three as the chakra of growth.

If you are ever seeking answers, remember that this is the chakra that will help open you to insight and soul evolution. Working with its energy can help you let go of habits and beliefs that do not serve you any longer.

All the forgiveness and letting go of emotions and thoughts that did not represent who I wanted to be and stood in the way of me hearing my soul were held in place because of the condition of the third chakra. It was time in my life for me to find my way back to the connection and magic. I did not want to settle for less or feeling mundane in my life. That was a third-chakra life lesson.

The fourth chakra is located at the heart. It is at the center of all of the seven chakras and of the human body. It is called *anahata* or the heart chakra. When we open this chakra, we are allowing ourselves to be an open flow of love, compassion, and acceptance of self and others. Openness here gives us the ability to forgive easily. This is my favorite chakra and it fully encompasses the saying, "Live from the heart."

I feel this is the chakra that opens us and unites us with the spiritual and the physical by bringing the spiritual to the physical. It is truly beautiful. Imagine the whole world opening this chakra—what a fabulous world it would be.

The fifth chakra is located at the throat. Known in Sanskrit as *vishuddha* ("purity") and it is the first of the three higher, spiritual chakras. Being in the throat region along with thyroid, jaw, and tongue it is related to our voice—both to how we speak and to how we listen and choose to express ourselves from our true selves or higher self. It is also the chakra of surrender. We surrender the old beliefs, habits in the third chakra and then open ourselves to our higher selves whose consciousness is connected to our heart chakra, and when we work with this energy we surrender our whole self to the higher self. All our expressions and creations now have deeper and more meaningful, loving purpose.

The sixth chakra, *anja* in Sanskrit, is often referred to as the third eye chakra because it is located between the eyebrows on the forehead. *Anja* means the "command center." When we are living from our true selves this chakra gives us divine perception and understanding. It is the chakra of light.

Anja chakra can help us to open to six spiritual gifts: imagination, intuition, perception, reasoning, memory, and the will. As we open this chakra, we open to divine guidance with trust. Our perception is now from a higher understanding, which also affects our reasoning, imagination, and memory. We also trust our intuition, which is one of the main ways our soul communicates with us.

This is the chakra I always want to keep fully open. I want to live in continual conversation with my soul.

The seventh chakra, aka the crown chakra or *sahas-rara*, is located on top of the head and is associated with our connection to the Divine/God. It is said to be a thousand-petal lotus chakra. Sahasrara is our ultimate enlightenment and full spiritual connection to everything that is.

When we open this chakra, we discover the ultimate truth that we are all one consciousness. We have a complete connection to everything and nothing. We are expansive beyond all time. And we realize that the most important aspect of our time on earth is the time when we immerse ourselves in love. Not just romantic love or parental love, but love of life and of each other as spiritual beings.

The concept of unconditional love is unfamiliar in our society. Some of us have not ever felt unconditional love in our lives. The love I received while growing up felt very conditional. Love was felt when I did what someone else wanted me to do. If I did not do what they wanted, then there did not seem to be very much love or understanding.

Unconditional love is different from romantic love. In fact, romantic love is often conditional. If that perfect someone has a habit you don't like, it's a deal breaker and you take your love back. If you do something your beloved doesn't like, your love can be gone in a jiffy.

By contrast, unconditional love involves acceptance of what is and allowing ourselves to see the beauty of other people. It depends on our ability to let go of judgment and expectation and instead appreciate them for the spirits and people they genuinely are.

Most people who open and balance this chakra have worked through the healing of the consciousness of the lower chakras: They've gone from "I"/"we" to letting go and evolving, and they've discovered the soul or true self. By this point in their awakening process, they are ready to let go of identifying with the physical body and the ego, and even with the reasoning intellect, in order to gain trust enough to move past identification with the individual soul to identify with God, the Beloved, or the expansive spiritual energy of the entire Universe. That is why the symbol of the heart chakra is a thousand-petaled lotus. This plant grows in swampy, muddy water and yet produces a strong, beautiful flower.

When my shaman friend explained the chakra system to me, I understood that, indeed, I had been working through each of my lower three chakras. My healing had begun with honoring myself and coming back to my "I," my relationship with my soul, which had involved healing my first chakra. Finding a way to live in the world had involved the second chakra. Then, identifying which of my beliefs did not serve me and clearing strong emotions lingering inside me from childhood that had involved the third chakra. Still, according to my friend, I would need to take a journey inside myself to entirely heal these emotions and let them go once and for all! This, I was told, would be the next step of my journey.

Okay, so I understood where I was spiritually. Now, it was time to do the work.

I tried to use a simple self-observation meditation I had used before to release my emotional residue, however I found it difficult because sometimes I wasn't even sure what was creating an emotion. This made it very difficult to work backwards from an event. Details of the actual events that had upset me were difficult to recover as it had been a long time in some cases, and also because I am very good at shoving things far down inside me.

I was more successful with a new meditation my friend told me about. I do not think it has an official name; personally, I just think of it as a healing meditation. Whenever I do this healing meditation, I allow myself to totally relax and, when ready, ask the anger and hurt I feel "Why do you feel this way? What is your story?"

Notice that I am in the position of observing and not getting involved with the emotion itself.

The first time I tried healing meditation, an emotion appeared to me as myself when I was seven years old. Once I discovered this little girl, I listened to her tell me her story. She talked about the priest saying her spiritual gifts were all in her imagination and asking her why she had allowed herself to concentrate on such "evil" things. And—*bingo*—there it was, the one phrase the priest had said that was stuck in my heart: "You have a wild and evil imagination that must be tamed." Oh, the anger I felt! How dare he criticize my imagination! I was not evil. And I did not need my imagination tamed. UGH!

To be completely honest, I did not get any further in meditation on that occasion. I felt as if I had opened a Pandora's box of anger. I realized I was supposed to stay detached. Oh well, that did not happen. I decided to take the rest of the day just to allow myself to feel and process the hurt. I ranted and reveled in disbelief at the priest's ignorance until I wore myself, and the anger, out!

That evening, I did the same meditation. Again, I visited my anger and hurt. Again, I heard the story. However, this time I was ready to accept it and talk to my little self. From conversing with the energy of the emotion, I learned that my priest did not know what he was doing. He did not know what I had experienced, or that goodness can come to everyone in the shape of angels and gifts. He was limited by his beliefs of what's right and wrong. My experience lay outside of his belief system—although not outside mine.

At last, I could allow myself to fully forgive the priest and disperse the heavy energy in my heart—offering it up to the Universe and allowing the story to leave my thoughts, and me, at peace. It felt amazing!

Allowing myself the time to cleanse the anger through venting had helped me to prepare for forgiveness. I had to dig the pain out from the depth of me, to allow it to surface so I could face it. If I had not allowed this to happen, my attempt to forgive would have been for nothing. The whole emotion had to leave me so I could gain freedom.

Forgiveness gives you the freedom to fly. It lightens your being.

I have known many people who did not feel that the subject of their wrath deserved forgiveness. If they ask my opinion, I will ask them, "Do the people who hurt you care what you are thinking? Are they suffering because you are angry at them?"

The usual answer is, "Not really!"

If the person we're mad with isn't being affected by the anger we feel, then who is being affected? We are. Our anger hurts us more than it hurts them.

The priest who judged me died some years ago. Why was I holding on to the anger and hurt? Who was it serving? And even more important, who was it hurting? It was hurting me.

Once I forgave the priest for defaming my imagination, I began to hear the small voice of my soul speaking to me more robustly. The heaviness in my heart was gone.

Forgiving Yourself

Forgiving another person or an event—someone or something external is never easy. However, we are generally willing to take on the task of forgiveness after we have processed our pain for a while. But what about forgiving ourselves? Why does this feel so much harder to do?

Did you know that holding on to guilt or other damaging thoughts about ourselves can affect our relationships, our careers—and every other aspect of our lives? When we hold on to these emotions, they get lodged in our muscles and change our chemistry of our bodies down to the cellular level. Frankly, not forgiving ourselves can destroy our health and well-being. There is absolutely no way to reach our full potential in any area if we feel guilty, ashamed, or angry at ourselves.

I believe forgiving ourselves is more difficult than forgiving others because we often feel we deserve to feel these destructive feelings. Sometimes we haven't even done anything offensive and yet guilt was laid on us as we were growing up by our parents or teachers. If you discover this is true for you, it is time to let go!

As the old saying goes, there is no use crying over spilled milk. You cannot go back in time and change whatever you are blaming yourself for having done. You can only move forward in a wiser and better way.

When I was in graduate school, I came across a stray dog with a broken leg. She was a beautiful and gentle dog and I immediately fell in love with her. But because I was living in student housing where no animals were allowed and I didn't know a vet or have enough money to pay for the medical bills, I called the Humane Society to come get the dog. My hope was that she would get the treatment she needed for her leg and find a home with a loving family. The next morning, I awoke with a sense of dread that I had made the wrong decision. I was ready to move off campus and somehow convince a vet to help me care for the dog. But when I arrived at the shelter to adopt this loving animal, I was told that she had been put down. It hadn't even been a full day!

I was crushed with sorrow and guilt. It was as if I had put the dog down myself. It took me a full week to stop blaming myself—or so I thought.

In reality, years later I still found that I could not even think about this poor, gentle creature without experiencing pangs of sadness and guilt. Although I am an animal lover, I wasn't even able to take on a dog or cat when I was financially able, because of remembering the choice I made. What if I chose wrong again?

A wonderful friend finally helped me to realize that I had to forgive myself so I could move on. I had to let go of the guilt. This was the best advice I have ever received. I remember sitting under a shady tree on a hot, sunny day talking out loud first to my memory and then to the spirit of this incredible animal. Yes, I had chosen wrong, but it was because I did not know or understand what the consequences of my choice would be. I truly had done what I thought was for the very best.

Understanding this mistake, I vowed to myself that in the future I would always check on the true nature of services for animals before calling upon an organization for its help. I then closed my eyes and met with my dog friend and asked her forgiveness for my bad choice. Finally, I released the guilt for good.

Because I released this guilt, I now have had many animals that I have saved, healed, found homes for, and even released back into the wild. If I had not released the guilt none of this would have happened.

No one deserves to be a slave to guilt or other negative emotions. Heal your pain by letting it go! Use it as a teacher. We are here to learn. Some of the lessons are hard, and yes, we can make wrong choices or act in wrong ways. However, the best we can do is to learn, heal, and let go. Then we are free to create something wonderful from our new knowledge.

This is what life is truly about: experiences and growth.

Sometimes we revel in the fire of anger, indignation, even righteousness. We love the feeling of being alive and taking action. When we are angry, our minds become highly focused and we feel charged with vital energy. This is a very addictive state of being.

And why would it not be? The law of polarity teaches us that opposites feel the same and are defined by their polar pair. Fear defines love and love defines fear. They carry the same amount of energy, just expressed differently.

Love is open, free, happy, and life altering.

Fear is closed, limiting, sad, and life altering.

I would love to say that I forgive with ease and always have that freedom of destructive anger under control. However, I am human! I have lived a life of much learning, which involved enduring the anger of others along with being angry with myself. In my unhappy marriage, it was the anger I felt that seemed to give me something to hold on to. It felt better to me than the mundane boredom and endless repetition did.

However, during my divorce, I quickly learned that anger, guilt, and even victimhood blinded me to what was really going on. Through indulging our emotions, my husband and I were building a bigger fire and prolonging our divorce. This was a firsthand lesson which taught me that if I could just forgive and let go, it would change everything.

My counterpart in the fight seemed to have less power over me the more I let go of anger. And then he began to see that stoking the fire in his belly was an ineffective tactic. By dropping my side of the fight, I was able to begin to focus on what really mattered, which was making sure my children were alright.

With each step of forgiveness that I took, I gained more freedom from attack. I began a ritual of sending loving light to my ex-husband while I continued growing my inner connection with my soul.

I feel strongly that everything we go through in our journeys of life has a lesson for us. These lessons are bigger than ideas like "I will never date anyone like that again" or "I will never trust again." Those types of lessons are based on the emotions of anger or hurt and are part of the critical mind. If we allow ourselves to really open ourselves to our feelings about a painful experience, forgive, and let go, we learn the lessons of the Universe and gain a higher understanding that we can use as we move forward.

I gained more power and freedom by choosing to focus on love than I would have had, if I continued to focus on the emotions of anger and fear that are its opposites. Granted, these are different energies. I always equate love with water and anger with fire. Yes, water is gentler, however it is flexible and moves freely. The key is that water puts out fires and fire cannot spread in water.

Please remember, forgiveness and emotional healing do take time, so we must have patience for ourselves. We heal in a time span that's our own, which is perfectly okay. Just wanting to heal is a huge step and will begin the process of forgiving. Understanding that this is just a step and gives us freedom so we can connect to something bigger in life also helps. A life of love and happiness and connection to soul is patiently waiting for us on the other side of forgiveness.

SKILLS FOR YOUR JOURNEY

Here are some additional ideas, concepts, or exercises you can try to have more flow in your personal journey. They'll help you to drop your baggage and find your way back to living with your soul.

- **When you're angry, encircle the target of your upset with loving white light.** This powerful little exercise, which will bring you relief, is best done either after a great meditation or writing your gratitude list for the day, or even after having some fun—after any experience that puts you in an emotionally uplifted state. Simply close your eyes, take a few deep, relaxing breaths, and then visualize someone with light surrounding them like a bubble.

  When I feel good, I think of things I love, like my family, my dogs and cat, and my friends, and I send them beautiful white, loving light. I watch this light surround and encircle them. Then I slip in the person I am most irritated with at that time, encircling them with the same loving white light. Try this yourself. While you're at it, take a few moments and surround yourself with some loving light too.

- **Remove the chains around your heart through forgiveness.** What has put its chain around your heart? Perhaps a situation that happens over and over or a pattern of sabotage that erupts when you try to achieve something meaningful? Maybe you simply don't feel excited or truly grateful for anything. Maybe you have buried feelings of hurt, disappointment, and anger deep inside you and they won't stay buried. Whatever is bugging you, in order to have a full connection with your soul, you must dig down and open those feelings up so you can understand, forgive them, and let them go.

Once you have discovered—or perhaps you have long known—what is blocking you from evolving emotionally, schedule a specific time to deal with it using the healing meditation described earlier in this chapter.

In a nutshell, the process is to allow hurt, anger, or guilt to surface, to understand the story, forgive whomever you feel needs the forgiving, stop blaming (someone else or yourself—or both), and release it to the Universe. This is a great process to rid the whole body of the energy.

- **Look for the spiritual lessons in your experiences.** Every experience we live through has a lesson for our souls. Once we have forgiven, we can open ourselves to the lesson. The lesson is almost always in a positive form. An example would be if I forgive and release the emotion that arises in response to someone betraying me. This forgiveness and releasing the story, allows me to open my mind to questions and thoughts that help me evolve and learn.

Under such circumstances I would ask: *What was going on in our relationship that he felt he needed to look elsewhere? Why did I not see the signs before the problem?*

What can I do in my next relationship that creates more love and happiness? Can you see how by releasing the emotions associated with the event of a betrayal you will gain the open-mindedness and power you need to have the relationship of your dreams.

Once we learn the true lesson underlying an experience, we never will experience that same lesson again.

Chapter 8

Bringing Soul into My Every Day

"Hello Soul. Are you there?"
"Of course, Alena. I am here." I am filled with peace!

Now that I am freer than I ever have been, I am open to hearing the guidance of my soul with clarity and open belief. No more will past experiences interfere with what I am able to hear from my soul and the Beloved. I genuinely want guidance, not because I want to evade responsibility for my life. In fact, it takes responsibility to decide to learn, let go, and grow/evolve. What I have always wanted is to bring magic back into my life and so I can think from a higher perspective. I want to feel soulful, spiritually connected in my everyday life.

The best example of this guidance was when my sixteen-year-old son told me on the way to school at 7:40 am that he wants to drop out of high school. *Seriously?*

First off, I am not a morning person. I am doing everything I can to get my boys to school. Second, I come from a family that very much believes in higher education.

In all honesty, while I was growing up, I had no idea what people without degrees did with their lives. My parents let it be known there was no way other than college. Period.

Another thought running through my head was that this high school was the second my son attended. We had started him out in the same private high school both his brothers attended. He was not happy there, so we transferred to the public school, but now there we sat in the car, deciding yet again how he could survive school.

With all the thoughts associated with my old conditioning running through my mind, I could have yelled, "What are you thinking? You can't go to college if you don't finish high school. We are a family that goes to college. What are you going to do with your life?"

I restrained that impulse. Not only would I have sounded like my parents if I did that, but also, I don't think it would have helped the situation.

Instead, I became quiet and asked my soul to give guidance. My soul said, "Look in his eyes. There is a better way." When I glanced in my son's eyes, I saw pain—true unhappiness. Because of this pain, I said to him, "Honey, go to school today. It will be your last day. By this afternoon we will have come up with another way for you to get a high school diploma."

Now, do you think I knew what I was going to do? NO! But I chose to go with the guidance I had asked for and received from my soul. I had to just believe in it.

I dropped my son off for school and went home to do some research. My goal was to build an unconventional structure for a high school education that he could succeed at with ease and joy. By noon I had found him three online schools for us to choose among, along with setting him up with a tutoring program and a counselor so he would have someone neutral, other than me, to talk to if needed. With these support systems in place, I was feeling much better about the situation, and I thanked my soul for helping me every step of the way as I developed this solution.

Four months later, my son was getting straight As, was happy, and he had friends and a girlfriend that I liked very much. And what I treasured the most was that my son totally trusted me to be there for him in his time of need. He now listens deeper when I speak and really helps me out around the house more because of how I listened to him and responded as his parent. This whole experience brought us a new level of connection and brought our whole family closer.

Every time I ask and listen to the guidance from my soul, things turn out better than I could ever imagine. So why do I forget to be open to this guidance until I really need it?

Sometimes it can be days or weeks before any of us—me included—remembers to say, "Hello, Soul. Are you there?" Of course, life gets busy and sometimes we fall back into the habit of listening to our critical mind or our reliance on an old belief system. We like to think we have it all under control—and most of the time, we do.

However, we should ask more often.

Because when we open to the soul and believe totally in the guidance we receive, everything works out even better than it does when we wrestle with our issues all on our own.

I think this reverting to old habits is because we have limited our imaginations by relying on our past experiences or what we have learned from others. As separate individuals, we do not have the vastness of mind as the entire Universe or our souls (which are tapped into cosmic wisdom).

Speaking for myself, every time I listen to my soul and follow its guidance things turn out better than I ever dreamed they would.

Routines with my Soul

After learning how to forgive people from the past and clearing my old belief systems, I decided to build my days around guidance from my soul. That means I scheduled different exercises in my calendar and created a routine with which I made sure I opened myself to connection with my soul, the Universe.

I have grown to love this morning routine, and if I ever miss doing some of it, I feel off somehow and uncentered for the rest of the day.

Because most of us never learned to connect to our souls in a way that we actually can talk to them and hear a response, we have to create our own special ways to open our minds and hearts to the small, loving voice of the soul. Without developing such methods, we risk becoming wrapped up in the mundaneness of doing what is expected or wanted of us, or anything we feel is needed. And once we begin practicing these methods, we need to be super consistent in doing them, otherwise everything will revert to being automatic and predictable. It is up to us to form new habits, mindsets, and even listening skills. It is up to us to take the responsibility to open ourselves so we can embody the soul.

I took this responsibility to heart. I really wanted a magical life—I wanted to live a life like I did as an unconscious competent in my younger days. Except this time, I wanted to be conscious and enjoy even more the experience of little miracles, moments of surprising ease and amazement. So, I created steps to open myself to my soul throughout the day. As a result, not only did I connect to my soul more and more every day, I also found that I was much more present. By which, I mean, I was surrendering to the guidance of my soul, allowing my attention to be on what was happening and fully enjoying and creating at that moment. Whether I was with my children, listening to music, or speaking to someone, I was totally present for that timespan and undistracted. This was a special gift.

But it was not just presence that I was seeking, although being present felt nice. No, I wanted something bigger.

As an unconscious competent in my younger life, whenever I was doing one thing only that one thing would be on my mind. All worries and to-do-lists vanished while I worked on the object of my focus. For instance, when I worked with a choir, every part of my mind, body, and soul was with the choir. If I was studying, again every part of me was into the subject I was studying.

The ability to focus like this is huge! When we are totally present with everything that it is, we hold on to nothing—there is no past or future for us. We are just there, enraptured with the moment. If there is a problem at home or with money, it vanishes from our consciousness and we don't have a care in the world. That's the reason my life as an unconscious competent was magical. I did not let any problem in my life hold me back—heck, I didn't even focus on problems most of the time because I was too busy experiencing life.

The greatest thing in the world is when our problems are solved with ease. Mine were, I think because I expected that they would be.

Thoughts create our emotions and the emotions along with our actions send the message of what we want to create in our lives to My Beloved and the Universe, which is the source of every manifestation. When people talk about the law of attraction—a well-known phenomenon in our universe—they are specifically talking about keeping the vibration of their personal energy high or happy so that they may attract something positive that is matching.

Everything in the cosmos—all matter and nonmatter, including human beings—is energy and, therefore, has a vibration. Different objects vibrate at different frequencies. Our emotions and our thoughts also vibrate.

Our emotions have many frequencies, which change depending on what we are thinking and experiencing. A sad emotion vibrates slowly and creates a field that is close to the physical body, whereas a happy or excited emotion vibrates quickly and creates a field that extends far from the physical body.

When we are content, peaceful, happy, or believe without a doubt in our abilities, then we can manifest the things we want to have or be with ease because the Universe always gives us back things whose vibration matches the one that we are radiating. This is the law of attraction. The ability to leave our cares behind and let the magic of the present moment lift our mood, says to the Universe, "I love this moment! I want more of this same type of high-frequency fun and purpose."

You can test this assertion out for yourself. Walk into a coffee shop or somewhere that people know you. One day walk in sad or upset—what happens? Next day, walk in happy and see if something different happens. Do people treat you differently?

Personally, I can't think of a better way to live my life than being happy and connected. Of course, you can understand all the reasons why. For me, it just feels good!

The Magical Morning Connection Routine

The first thing I do as I get out of bed every day—even on the weekend—is say, "Good morning, Soul. Thank you for this fabulous day to be and serve." I then practice some stretching or yoga. During the week, if there is a shortage of time, I dress and drive my youngest to school, while my middle son begins his day with the computer school. After my youngest is dropped off, I either go home and get comfortable on the porch or pick up a tea and drive to my favorite natural spot. When settled in one of these places, the porch or out in nature, I begin forming a magical connection with deep breathing and writing my gratitude list.

I begin by writing down "Thank you." Below this, I then list five to ten things in my life that I feel extremely grateful for. As I list each item, I picture it in my mind and allow myself to feel emotion filling my body. For instance, if I write that I am grateful for my children, then I see a clear picture in my mind's eye of all of us together having fun, laughing, and thriving. This fills me with joy!

This technique is so important for forming a solid connection with my soul in the morning because it is much easier for me to hear my soul when my mind has been opened by gratitude and wonder. If I am sad or in a hurry, then the critical mind takes over or I begin to think too much in the future about things that need to get done. The soul can only be heard when we are present and open to receiving. Gratitude starts my day off with the best of my life and puts me in the best of the present. But I always carry my gratitude pad with me as I move through the world.

Next, I get quiet, close my eyes, and ask my soul and the Universe for any messages for the day. Sometimes I don't hear anything right at that time, so I just enjoy the peace. To connect with the soul, we simply ask , "Are you there, Soul?" and wait for a response. It may take a few times however, we will begin to hear a soft voice filled with peace enter our ears or minds.

It is important to remember that our soul and the Universe are always trying to send us messages if we ask—it is only we who ever shut down the connection. If you cannot hear the soul, then you must open yourself to hearing it another way. Do not stop trying to hear it outright. Be patient because there may be a period of transition before you get good at listening. Maybe you'll keep seeing the same animal or one exhibiting unusual behavior. Or maybe the words of a particular song that you suddenly hear apply to your life. My favorite type of message is when I am talking with someone and, out of the blue, they say something out of character—however, the comment applies to my life or a decision I have to make.

We must stay open in observing after we ask to be connected because the soul will reach out to us in any way that it finds us to be open to it.

After asking for a message, I then send loving light to three or more people or situations that have caused me conflict or difficulty. I like to close my eyes and visualize the light surrounding and comforting them.

Finally, I take out my calendar. Though I have my schedule set for the day already, I take out a piece of paper or use the back of my gratitude list and write out my schedule by hand again. Why? Because, as I write it by hand, I am thinking, *Who do I want to be while I accomplish this day?* Being as opposed to doing. For instance, if I anticipate that the day is going to be very full and busy, I will think of how calmly I will face it. This step in the process helps me focus and establish an intention for myself. I am now ready for the day to begin.

Transforming the Mundane to Magic

During the day I always take time to see the wonder and feel grateful. I did this even when I was young. There is so much to wonder or awestruck about. I personally love looking at the sky because it's always a gift—always different and always beautiful. It's as if the Universe have taken up their paint brushes and co-created a painting. Or I will notice the beauty in someone or what that person is creating in his or her life.

How the human mind works is amazing, particularly how it can be opened to perceive more than just the self. When we step out of ourselves to look at the wonders of our world then we begin to open our minds to perceive the Universe and our souls. It is amazing what wonderment enables us to do. Not only do we hear or feel the soul when we're open, we also can receive messages from our surroundings. Messages can come to us in the words of a song, in an animal that presents itself to us, or maybe through something someone says. Opening to the signs of the Universe throughout the day keeps us awake to the magic.

What about the Fun?

One of my favorite ways to keep my connection open is to add a bit of fun to my day every day. Sometimes I plan it and sometimes it is impromptu. I may be driving and suddenly see a road I have never explored, or venture into a bookstore—one of my most favorite places to be. I always find a great book or magazine, grab a cup of tea, and just allow my mind to create. Curling up with a book is my happy place. Or sometimes it is rocking out to my favorite music with my very own creative dance moves. This is always fun because my dogs like to join me.

I have found that having fun doesn't have to be something big—although I do enjoy being with friends and enjoying idea-provoking conversations with them. The everyday type of fun of small little moments I manufacture just for myself puts a smile on my face and allows me to feel like a kid again. This could mean doing something as simple as listening to my favorite musical artist and allowing myself to totally get into the music. Or it can be finding time to watch a movie that I have wanted so much to see.

Yes, I realize that some days can seem crazy—which is when I must deliberately make the time for some fun. A perfect example is the Saturdays when my children were younger. I used to be a cab driver for my children with their active schedules from 9:00 am to 3:00 pm every Saturday. All I did those days was drive my kids to different events, like sports, or birthday parties. It was awful!

On one particular Saturday, my oldest son got into the car and said, "Mom, I need to be dropped off at my friend's house first and then taken over to the school." His friend lived twenty minutes from the school and thirty minutes from where we currently were located. Once I heard the reason for the stop, I agreed that we did have to visit his friend; however, making this extra visit did not make me happy. It wasn't going to be fun.

"Okay honey, but we need to stop at the coffee shop first," I said, already feeling a little lighter at the thought of it.

"Mom, we don't have time. I need to be at school soon," my son replied with urgency.

"I know. This will only take a minute and I need to stretch," I said as I turned into the coffee shop.

"You're getting out of the car?" Now he was totally astonished.

I laughed, got out of the car, and walked into the coffee shop. My mind suddenly felt good. I was going to get my favorite drink, talk to some people, and enjoy the music and connection inside. I was going to have a bit of fun just for me right that minute. I spotted some friends sitting at a table in the corner, so I chatted with them while I waited for my fat-free latte to be prepared by the barista. I was feeling good.

Once my latte was ready, then it was time to go. I felt much better, more grounded and like I could deal with the rest of my cab-driving duties; however, I decided things were going to change in the car also.

I walked back to the car and got in with my son who was waiting impatiently for me. I started the car, then turned on some music I knew both of us really liked and began to sing. Soon his head started to nod to the music, then he was singing too, and before you knew it, we were giving our own full-blown car concert! Carpool karaoke!

As kids we are taught that work comes first and fun later. But this does not have to be the case. If we are having fun while working or during our breaks, this can help us stay more productive and creative. Why? Because we have renewed focus and clarity. The fun activates our imaginations.

When we activate the imagination, we are using one of the six gifts of the soul. And remember, the soul is only ever interested in expansion, creation, and love. When we are having fun, we are creating something, whether that is friendship, accomplishment, or a new level of our personal self.

Our responsibility is to take steps to lighten our hearts and open our minds, which allows the imagination to begin creating the fun, which in turn lightens us more and keeps us centered in the present moment.

And that is when the voices of our souls can be heard.

I like to think of moments of fun as me tickling my soul, so it wants to sing and play with me.

The Free Will Rule

Throughout the day I am always asking, "Are you there, Soul?" or "What do you think, Soul?" In other words, I am always asking for the channel of connection between myself and my soul to be open. This is important because we have free will. The Universe and our souls cannot and will not just take over running our lives for us.

We come to this planet for a reason. And even if we do not remember what the reason is, we are still learning how to fulfill our purpose. How we go about this is up to us—this too is a lesson. The Universe cannot take away our freedom of choice or decision unless we ask, and even then, the answer is only ever a suggestion and never an order. This means the Universe can only step in and help us if we ask.

For this reason, every morning when I rise, I ask, "How may I serve today? Or "How can I make a big splash for the best for all today?" I am inviting guidance—choosing to hear from my soul. It is my choice when and how to connect.

I have learned the hard way that there are always several roads leading to the same destination—my lessons on this planet. Some roads are long and difficult, others long but fun.

Some roads are full of ease and flow, fast and dynamic. The one time I chose to listen to other people telling me what road to take in my life, my decision led me on a long and difficult road. I learned valuable lessons by taking that road; however, I know in my heart that those same lessons could have been learned with more ease, flow, and fun.

Every time I listen to my soul and my heart—which really is very well connected—I am choosing the road that I was always meant to be on. The discovery of the ideal path is fun, and I know I have found it when there is ease and flow in every step.

Sometimes I allow my ego or critical monkey mind to push and want everything to happen NOW. This usually takes me temporarily off my chosen path and signals resistance to the Universe, which of course, then makes the road harder. The faster I recognize the ego has become involved and notice how hard my path is becoming, I simply correct my thinking and begin to open more to my soul. I do not punish myself.

Through staying in touch with my soul I learn about the bigger picture of my life, meaning, I see the possibilities and the abundance I am already enjoying now and over time this has made me trust that the guidance I receive is accurate.

What I love the most is that I am never alone. I never have to suffer from doubt or anguish over a decision. Whenever I feel unsure of what to do, I quiet myself and ask for advice. If an answer doesn't come, no problem. I have learned that messages can and do come in many ways throughout the day. The uncertainty will go away once I get the guidance.

Whenever I feel tightness in my stomach, it usually means something isn't right. Again, I will ask, "What is it you are trying to tell me, Soul?" And I get a new answer. In this way, I quickly learn why my intuition has been activated.

I realize this sounds so funny because we are our souls. We are souls with bodies not bodies with souls. So, why do we have to ask? (I have often asked myself this question.) Do we become separated from our souls as a result of trying to assimilate into society? Does the critical mind become so strong and loud for most of us that we mistakenly think we are the critical mind?

As I find myself connecting more to my soul, I find it harder to listen to the voice of the critical mind. It is so loud, negative, and judgmental. I realize that the critical mind has a tricky consciousness and will evolve as I evolve. Because I have created a firm connection to my soul, which will always tell me the truth, I know I will be able to tell when the critical mind is present and telling me its evolved falsehoods.

Each day, as I keep practicing my connection techniques, I feel more like my soul. I find that I am grateful throughout the day without even trying. My mind is light and happy, and I have a firm belief that everything will be fine. Days and days may go by before I notice that there has been no doubt in my life. It is as if all the complications I used to experience are gone. How silly the doubt was anyway!

Best of all, I am seeing a change in the people around me. My children are much more relaxed and happier too. They are coming to me with their thoughts and problems because I am seeing everything from a bigger viewpoint. I don't get upset easily and we have honest and respectful dialogues. They enjoy spending time with me. What amazing gifts!

I knew that life would change for me on this journey of connection to my soul, but I didn't realize there would be life changing ripple effects for everyone around me. Lately, I am finding that most people feel at ease around me, trust me more, want to talk to me, or just to sit with me quietly together. They feel the vibration of my soul.

It makes me so happy to see them fill with ease and relaxation when they sit with me, and I want to let them know that their whole lives could be this way!

Now that I am stronger in my connection and loving every day, it is time for the next step in my journey. This will be interesting for me!

SKILLS FOR YOUR JOURNEY

Here are a few ways I have learned to maintain a full connection to my soul and keep my life vibrant and joyful along with peace with my soul leading the way. These skills fill my life with discovery, happiness, and meaningful connection to people and the world.

Remember that all my exercises in this book are for you to try so that you may slowly adapt to a new way of being. Continue doing those which work best for you.

- **Form a magical morning connection.** Try starting your own day with the morning connection routine and then adapt it to your lifestyle and ways of being.

My magical morning connection takes about twenty minutes. Yours should also be about that long to be really effective.

1. Write a gratitude list of five to ten items, allowing yourself to feel emotions.
2. Ask your soul for a message.
3. Send loving white light to surround three or more people or situations.
4. Review your day's to-do list while asking: *Who do I want to be while I accomplish this day?*

If this works for you as is, that's great. However, if you want to add something or change a step that would be fine. Just remember that a morning connection needs to have at least these four components:

1. Expressing gratitude.
2. Connecting with a higher force, like your soul.
3. Setting an intention to bring good into the world.
4. Gaining a clear focus or intention for the day.

- **Take time to see the wonders of the world.** Set a goal to see or experience three beautiful things or things that give you a feeling of awe during the day. This tip will refocus your mind so that you are not always simply being busy. By filling your mind with wondrous images, you will empower yourself to focus in a more creative and open way on your career, job, parenting . . . whatever.

- **Deliberately add fun to your day.** This is an important skill because many of us take life too darn seriously. To remedy the problem of seriousness, you must (at least at first—until it is second nature) plan the fun. For the next week or two plan a bit of fun every day. It doesn't have to be a big thing; it just has to be something you find refreshing to do that makes you smile, lighten up, and enjoy the moment! Soon you won't have to plan the fun. Your mind, body, and soul will expect it. I have gotten to the point now that if something isn't fun I look for some fun in doing it or I don't do it at all. Fortunately, I can make almost anything fun! My whole being expects it.

  Once you open to fun, you will laugh about how serious you always were and some of the serious wrinkles on your face will begin to fade. Of course, some things in life are serious; but really, almost everything doesn't have to be as serious as we treat it. Once you wake up to understanding this perspective, your life will take a dramatic turn for the better and hearing your soul will become a hundred times easier.

Chapter 9

Please Come Back, Soul

Our souls want to feel safe. If a soul does not feel safe,
part of it or all of it may leave.

Forgiveness is for us, not for the person we are forgiving.
We are the ones holding the energy of anger, hurt, or
whatever in our bodies.

Every part of the body holds memory. Our brains release
chemicals that correspond to different thoughts and emotions,
affecting our organs, joints, bones, and muscles. We especially
can feel how our muscles hold on to emotions, giving us tension in our shoulders, backs, jaws, and so forth. This can cause
serious, chronic health problems if stress chemicals flood the
body consistently. Every time we recreate a scene that caused
us pain in our thoughts, the feeling feeds the brain instructions on what to do and the same chemicals are released again.

When I am remembering situations of anger or where my fight-or-flight instinct was triggered, then I release cortisol and adrenaline from my adrenal glands. In response, my body shuts down the functioning of my digestive tract and other organs because it is getting ready to do something dramatic to rescue me from danger. Some people suffer from adrenal fatigue, a condition where the adrenal gland can become magnified. It can begin to misfire during the night, causing the heart to race and anxiety to set in. A factor that may cause this to happen is holding on to the emotions of a situation related to a person whom they've never forgiven, rather than learning the lesson from the experience and letting the pain go.

Every physical condition has both a medical explanation and a spiritual explanation. What shamans teach is that the soul can decide that the environment we've created inside our body is not a place it wants to be anymore. Parts of our souls may decide to splinter off and depart for a safe refuge until we correct the environment within ourselves.

I knew something was a little unbalanced inside. Maybe my yin was not happy for a while however, I really think it was due to the last part of the marriage and the divorce.

I had just filed for the divorce. As I have stated before, it was a very difficult, hostile divorce. Although I was growing as a person and awakening my connection to my soul, the divorce proceedings and emotional attacks I was on the receiving end of got to be very distracting and difficult to endure. On my side of the breakup, I was doing my best to be forgiving and I kept asking My Beloved and the Universe for help to ensure that the result of my battle with my ex-husband would be for the betterment for all concerned, especially my children; however, I still sometimes felt distrust, along with downright fear and frustration, and would second guess my soul.

Back and forth from forgiveness and letting go, to a new legal assault from my adversary, new anger or fear, new confusion, and the need to refocus. My emotions at one point were changing almost by the minute. The almost every day trauma was not good for my mind, body, or spirit.

During this period, I took a trip to my home state of Vermont where I grew up. I love summers in Vermont—the cool mornings and evenings and warm days—and I needed this time away to unwind, refocus my mind, and look at things from a higher perspective. One late morning, as I walked down the brick sidewalk on Main Street past various cafés and charming stores, I came upon a sign for a person who can read your soul. I found this interesting since I was just beginning to discover my soul. I walked upstairs to the woman's office and signed up for a reading. Never would I have guessed what she would say to me or how it would affect my life on many levels.

I sat myself down in front of a tall, quiet woman with intense eyes. She studied everything about me without even a smile and then, with a heavy sigh, she sat down.

"Your soul is not complete. The little girl of your soul is sad and perplexed, and the boy is angry. One has left."

"Left? What do you mean? Why do I have two parts, or more, to my soul? How does just part of a soul leave?" I fired off my questions rapidly not understanding how this could be—wasn't my soul my essence? How could it just leave me?

"You are going through something in your life now that has made the feminine side of your soul very unhappy. The masculine side of your soul is angry because it did not have a voice and was very unhappy for a long time throughout your marriage," the reader replied very matter of fact, as if she wasn't surprised.

I left her office. She had to be crazy—my soul was a boy and girl? —this could not be true. This woman had said that my soul had many parts.

Shaking my head, I decided to put the reading out of mind until I could learn more about the soul.

Later that month, I met up with my shaman friend again. As we sat on the hillside looking over a flowery field of my sacred spot at the old monastery, I told him about the serious lady in Vermont who had told me about my poor half-soul. "Could what she told me be true?" I asked.

He assured me that it could. Our souls, he said, are both *yin* and *yang* or, as the serious lady in Vermont had said, female and male. When we go through a trauma or something that affects us deeply—it impacts our soul. If what we are going through is extremely difficult or prolonged, part of the soul can go into hiding.

My friend asked me a series of questions. Was I moving forward with confidence? In my marriage, had I felt as if something in my life got lost? Did I have more trouble looking within myself or executing my ideas recently? And lastly, did I feel that I was not myself in some way?

I explained that I was trying to move forward the best I could, although I felt like I was being held back. Something was keeping me from dealing with my situation in a confident and progressive way. And yes, my marriage did seem to have taken something from me. I did not feel the same way I did before I was married. The optimism, the belief I'd once had in myself was gone and I had lost my voice. I felt as if the world were spinning around me and I could not move, or like I had been tossed into a world that I did not understand or know how to navigate. Those days, I was watching my whole situation grow larger and I wasn't moving into action. Something was off. Where was me—the action taker?

My friend was watching me intently as I told him about my situation and how I was spinning my wheels ineffectively over and over. When I finished talking, he remained quiet for a little while. Both of us just looked out at the field moving with a peaceful breeze. Finally, he began to explain the soul from the shamanic perspective.

A Shaman's View of the Soul

The soul, like everything else in the cosmos, is guided by the law of polarity. This is the principle of opposites defining each other: Up defines down, high defines low, coldness defines hotness. For example, the coldness of ice defines what sitting in the sun getting hot is *not*. Pairs of opposites share characteristics of what they are and aren't.

One aspect of our souls is the blending qualities of yin and yang. Yin is the introspective polarity and brings us three of the six gifts of the soul: imagination, intuition, and perspective. It is the more feminine side of the soul. Yang is the action taking polarity. It also has three of the six gifts of the soul:

will, reasoning, and memory. It is the more masculine side of the soul. This is why the serious lady in Vermont had used the words *girl* and *boy* to define the two sides of my soul. She must have felt I would understand the polarity better.

My shaman friend interpreted the reading I had received for me. "The yin (female) part of your soul has hidden itself away. This creates an imbalance. The yin and yang parts of your soul depend on each other to give you effective guidance. Being unable to access all six of your soul's gifts could be causing you to feel incomplete like you are spinning your wheels, or even not progressing at all. This phenomenon of soul loss or absence is more common than you might think."

Listening to his explanation, I realized that it rang true. Yes, the yin part of my soul had left me and was hiding somewhere safe. The good news was that I could get it back. But my friend advised me, my feminine essence would only come back if I first created a safe environment for it to return to.

To understand better why my yin had left, I took a hard look at myself during my marriage. I estimated that for a greater percentage of my time as a married person, I'd had to be the strong one. I was the one who made most of the decisions. I had never felt that I could fully rely on my husband, along with the restrictions of no working outside the home and the type of friends I could have, my faith in my husband faded. Most of the time I felt very restricted and still making the decisions.

My soul's yin side never was able to feel secure, safe or at home in my marriage. I very rarely received the nurturing and support I needed, and the love I got seemed cold and conditional. I experienced this as indifference or not caring. My partner and I had different values. The concepts, issues, and ideas that I found important to our lives were not important to him. So, I chose to make myself busy doing anything I could to not notice the pain and unimportance I felt.

That's why I lost part of my soul and the magic in my life. Of course, my yin said good-bye!

Now it was time to call my yin back home, but what type of home would I provide for her? One thing was for sure, I could not keep ignoring her. This part of my soul had to have a voice and feel safe.

I decided it was time to create security and comfort in my life—starting within myself. If I felt good about myself, my world, my home, then my soul would be happy also. Even with all the insecurity from the divorce I was going to create an environment that yin would love to be part of. I was going to seduce her to come home to me. What did I feel I could do at this moment to begin? Build my belief in myself!

I began to look at parts of myself I had always been told were my faults. These so-called faults or criticisms of me had to go. Every time I made a move, in my head I would hear, "Alena, you are so bossy. Alena, you always have a crazy scheme. Alena, you are such a flower child—grow up!"

Were these faults *really* "faults"? What was wrong with being a flower child?

My love of life, nature, and people were assets. I should foster this love, not negate it and call it a useless fault. Yes, this love did allow me to see the good in people, and sometimes those same people were not so good. However, did that mean

I should be skeptical of others all the time? Maybe I could love them and understand that they could choose to shine with goodness or to act self-serving. Maybe my love could help them grow in love.

I saw that this could become my strongest gift and if I trusted it.

Each day, I would go to my sacred space and call up different criticisms of me that I had heard since childhood. I would talk through each one with my soul just as I had talked through my flower child fault. I found this process fun—like a game. How to take the negative and turn it into a strong positive. I wrote down all the positives. It made me feel good, free, and strong. By the time I finished, I felt like I was a pretty awesome person who had incredible gifts that had helped me all the way through my life even as I tried to push them away. Now I would actively use them!

I was excited to imagine what I could achieve.

I also decided to look at my finances and income. The lawyer for my divorce was expensive. I wanted to plan for my future, and I felt it was time for me to understand the finances I had never been allowed to know about during the marriage.

A third important life analysis I undertook was a look at how my children were handling the divorce and the tension between me and their father. That was an eye opener. They were having a hard time processing things. I began to pull us together and initiate open discussions, as well as giving them constant support and love. My soul helped me ensure they would be fine.

Finally, I decided to secure my home by taking in a dog orphan—my first big, red dog, Ralphie, who was also a fabulous judge of character and protector.

In every part of my life I had created the feeling that "yes, this is a safe and nurturing place to be."

So, did my yin half-soul just pop back in now that my home, finances, and family were squared away. No. Because that is not the way it works.

The way I got my yin half-soul back was to locate a teacher of shamanism who did soul retrievals. Once she learned how much I had improved myself and my environment, she became open to performing a beautiful ceremony for welcoming my soul home.

It is possible to call your soul home yourself, but I loved having a witness who could say with assurance, "It is solid. Your soul is home." It was beautiful how the little ceremony the teacher did seemed to seal the deal.

I loved the candle-lit room and lying peacefully, listening to the shaman drum and allowing my mind to relax and enjoy. She then took me to my soul, which was lying waiting under a seashell somewhere on an ethereal beach by the sea. I thought that visualization was very appropriate because I love the water. Together, the shaman and I called my missing soul fragment back into my body. Yin was home.

Immediately I felt a profound calmness within me. There was a sense of peaceful strength resting in the core of my body, an overwhelming knowledge that I and my family were fine and would be fine. Love seemed to fill every part of my being.

This was awesome!

Memories of my true character rushed into my mind. I recalled being the young woman who never said the word *can't* and who believed that all she had to do was try and it would happen the way it was supposed to happen—whatever that was to be. Always feeling that confidence that came from the calm strength. Feeling free to be curious!

I am BACK! I thought.

Never again was I going to allow myself to suffer so badly that my soul would leave.

My Conversation with All of My Soul

As soon as I got home, I went to my sacred space with pen and pad in hand, got myself comfortable, closed my eyes, and asked my whole soul, "What would my life be like if I honored you Soul, and what do you need to flourish?" Then I waited.

It did not take long for a response to come as my soul was eager to provide me with answers. What I heard was, "Get to know all of me, both the feminine (yin) part that is the dreamer inside me, and the masculine (yang) part that takes the dreams out into the world. Honor their gifts and knowledge. You are neither yin nor yang, you are both. Build a life that allows both aspects of your being to be heard and valued. Yin needs you to honor yourself, so the relationships you build should allow you to honor your inner essence, your soul."

"Okay, I understand somewhat. How do I know if someone I allow in my life gives me space to honor my soul? Isn't it just up to me?" I asked.

"By building a life with guidance by your soul, you will come to full understanding of who will respect you and your wishes. By honoring your soul and receiving its guidance, you won't choose the wrong partner again—you will know the next person you love is right for you and healthy to be around because the guidance will continue, and you will be happy, strong, and fully alive even when you are in this person's company. Alena, when your soul is complete it becomes your connection to the entire Universe."

"Thank you!" I replied, so very grateful for the wisdom. Never again would I lose such an important part of me because of a relationship.

Now that my soul was whole, I could hear it so much clearer than before, like it was stronger. I wasn't sure if this was the case or if I had only grown my confidence in hearing my soul. Really it did not matter. All of me was home and I felt like myself again.

On a side note, because I enjoyed my own soul retrieval so much, I asked this shamanic teacher to teach me how to retrieve souls for other people. Now I am able to create an incredible homecoming for anyone who wants to bring a fragmented piece of their soul home back from where it's hiding from them. What an awesome bonus for me.

SKILLS FOR YOUR JOURNEY

What an amazing journey it is to learn about your soul and gain a sense of completeness from having such a strong connection to your soul and the Universe. As you do the following exercises, remember that your success depends on how honest and whether you open up during the process. I really do not feel I could have been as open to the work of soul retrieval as I was if I hadn't done the early work to forgive. So, if you believe that you have any baggage still hiding deep inside you, go back and reread Chapters 7 and 8. The more objective and curious you are able to be, the more insight will be revealed to you.

- **Find out if you are missing part of your soul.** If you feel that you may be missing part of your soul, then ask yourself some of the questions that my shaman friend asked me.

  Are you moving forward in life with confidence?

  Did you have a trauma or difficult challenge, or were you in a long, stressful situation that left you feeling different inside?

  Do you have trouble looking within yourself or moving forward in creating a life you love?

  Finally, do you not feel like yourself totally? Is something inside you a little off kilter?

  If you answer yes to any of these questions, then it is possible that part of your soul may be in hiding. Really, only you can know! For me, it was obvious that something wasn't right because I wasn't feeling like that confident, happy woman. Instead, I was feeling and acting like a victim in my situation of the divorce. It was hard to stay above and see clearly. My point is: Something wasn't right. You will have to assess your own situation to determine if soul retrieval is needed.

It is important to note that not everyone is missing part of the soul.

- **Creating a home for your soul**. Let's face it, we feel good when our situation in life, health, and love is going well. But to be honest, this isn't usually the case. Most of the time, too many of us feel unhappy, flat, or stuck. We worry and believe things are impossible to accomplish. Even worse, we stay in toxic relationships and jobs far too long. We frequently take abuse—whether it's verbal, emotional, or physical—as if we are supposed to just suck it up without complaining. Sometimes we think we deserve it.

  It is time to wake up and take responsibility for creating an environment in which we can thrive and grow, where the soul is nourished. If we don't create it, then who will? This means, it is time to honor all parts of you and your life. Do an audit of your situation. Is there anything in your environment—at work or at home, with friends, family, or in your love life—that you want to improve? Is there a situation that you've been putting off dealing with? Where in your life have you not stepped up and taken the responsibility for making it better?

  Make a list of things that come to mind, and then commit to addressing them with guidance from your soul.

  It is immensely liberating to take responsibility for everything in your life. It frees up mental space and feels so good to have acted in a positive way.

Chapter 10
Flow Like Water

Here is an interesting story you may relate to: When I graduated from school with three degrees in music, my mother and father told me that they felt music was not a profitable career and tried to insist that I choose something else to do. But instead of acceding to their wishes, I decided to stay put. I did not want them to control my life.

Once I had defied my parents' wishes by not moving home, they cut me off from their financial help. That left me with $200 in my pocket and a few pieces of furniture. The problem was that I was close to being homeless and at a loss of what to do about it! How was I going to move forward without money, a job, or a home? How was I going to afford even the basics of life, like food? My mind was spinning with indecision.

To clear my head, I felt a deep desire to drive to my favorite park. People were walking, playing, laughing, and exploring its blooming flower gardens. What I wanted to do was to lay down and become one with the wide, beautiful river that flowed through the center of the park. As soon as I arrived, I could hear the water calling me.

I parked the car and walked right to the river's edge. All nature was alive around the water. A family of ducks was quacking as they paddled down the river in a straight line. A blue heron stood on a rock midriver, like a statue, waiting patiently for his food to swim by him. Birds sang, and squirrels played. I felt right at home.

I grew up on a large lake in the Northeast, where our lives revolved around beaches, nature, and incredible bodies of water. My fondest memories are of an area around a lake. Now, as I sat beside this wide, strong river, a deep peace settled over me like the comfort of the company of an old friend. I could breathe deeply again, and my shoulders finally let go. I could feel strength begin to flow back into my body. I could feel my mind clearing.

I began to reflect on the strength of the river. This strong, beautiful river had been abused by pollutants, overfished, dammed up, and then un-dammed again. No matter what was done to it, it continued to flow knowing that nothing would stop it from going to its destination.

There is tremendous strength from any body of water. However, there is also a gentleness and smooth flow. Water hypnotizes you if you watch it for a while.

The calm and steady strength of this river kept it flowing, providing life to every landscape it entered. Every animal in this park had made its home close to this river. Every bird that flew by stopped at this river on its migratory travels, and people came just to be close to it. It was the center of all life in the park.

Finally, a personal revelation hit me: If this river could keep flowing despite everything it had gone through, then I too could "be like a river and adapt." I saw that I could surrender and flow through my circumstances with trust and ease. I could continue to build a calm, strong inner core. Like the river, I could flow around the challenges and difficulties I encountered. I decided right then and there, sitting on a riverbank, that I would flow with strength toward my destination. I was empowered.

I walked back to my car to learn that I had received a phone message from a friend saying that she had found an apartment for me. All I needed was a down payment of money for the first and last month's rent. It was great news, except the amount she told me was way above what I could afford. At the end of her message, she asked, "Do you want to see it?" I looked back toward the river. Then, I phoned my friend and said, "Yes, I would like to see it."

I picked her up, and we drove to the apartment together. The neighborhood was filled with old homes and located only a block from the park where I had found my calmness and strength. I found that fact very interesting. When we arrived, we followed the landlord up a flight of stairs. As he opened the door, I fell in love. The place needed work; however, there was a little balcony off the kitchen. I saw myself sitting there each morning, a cup of tea in my hands, and with plants surrounding me. Oh yes, this was where I was supposed to be.

I asked the landlord about the cost of the rent. When he replied with the number beyond my reach, I quickly responded that the place needed work. To my surprise, I started talking about mold under the carpet and the need for fresh paint and weather-stripping of a window. Where was this coming from? I did not know anything about redoing apartments, but I heard myself say, "If you allow me to stay here for two months free and pay for all the supplies, I will pull up the carpet, redo the wood floors, and fix all the other problems in this apartment for you."

To my amazement, the landlord said okay. I was experiencing ease and flow! I now had the perfect place to live and was beginning the next chapter of my life.

My next step was to look for a job that would provide me good money, so I quickly could feel financially secure and free to start my dream job of teaching music at a university in the fall. The first newspaper I picked up had a listing for the perfect job, one that would give me the potential to make between $500 and $1,000 a week. I got the job! More ease and flow—I liked this!

To this day, I often go back and visit that beautiful river and thank it for providing me with the insight and clarity to start my life with strength, trust, and belief.

This experience proved to me that we can learn lessons from nature and the elements of the natural world.

Water is mentioned many times in *Tao Te Ching*, the Bible, Buddhist scripture, and the oral teachings of many pagan spiritual traditions.[4] I love the fact that water is universally associated with the giving of life, purity, and hope and health, perhaps because it is one of the most crucial elements for survival.

All nature, including water, can teach us about life if we simply open our eyes. Water may not have the explosiveness of fire or the immovable strength of a mountain, but it is more adaptable. Flowing water will find a way around any obstacle. It can create new pathways in rock and change form without losing its essence: It can be steam or liquid or ice, muddy or clear, deep or shallow, flowing or still, but it is always water. Water can nourish life or wash it away. It has so many energetic properties.

When I sat next to the river, the Universe offered me a variety of lessons. Of course, there was the lesson of the river water, which was where my attention went that particular day. Because of this, I trust that this was the lesson I needed most at that moment. However, there was also a blue heron near me, which, if I had chosen to watch it, might have taught me a lesson of patience and stealth. The squirrels might have taught me to lighten up and have the faith that all would fall in place as I walked forward.

My point is that the Universe speaks to us in every way it possibly can. We simply must get out of our heads and open our eyes and ears, so we don't miss its lessons.

Sound strange? Could it be possible that the Universe, the Divine, would find *you* in this massive world? Well, why not? You are worthy of attention.

A Gnostic Approach to Life

The Gnostics believed that the spirit of God—the Divine—was present in all living things and that we can perceive this presence in every leaf on a tree, every blade of grass, in the air we breathe, and in every cloud and raindrop. They knew it is present in all life.

Who were the Gnostics, and why should we care what they thought? Experts say that Gnosticism started in the Mediterranean region and Near East around the time of Christianity. Their communities flourished in roughly the first century of the common era (ce). Their beliefs dealt with the mystical, esoteric teachings of the Divine.

Along with the Gnostics, adherents of many other religions say that the Divine (call this intelligent energy by whatever name makes you feel the most comfortable) is omnipresent—meaning it is in all things everywhere. If this is true, why wouldn't the Divine also reside inside each one of us? Are we not part of everything?

And if Spirit is everywhere and part of us and everything else, then why wouldn't this physical world participate in guiding us and helping us evolve?

If this is the case, then we are offered guidance all the time. As we tap more and more into listening to the soul, we are creating a different world. We are becoming attuned to the divine presence and aware that there is more than meets the eye. When we open ourselves up to the soul, we begin to open ourselves to the Beloved and the Universe. We become stronger when living from our souls because we are living from divine guidance.

Guidance has always been there. But as we live better aligned with our souls, we become much more sensitive to what we need and the resources that are around us.

The day I went to the park, I knew that I was in my head too much. I was overly worried about not having money or a job. This recognition gave me a choice. I could stay in that worry and allow it to drive me crazy, or I could feel what my body was saying and open to the guidance of my soul, which was telling me, "Go to the river in the park!"

If I were totally in my critical mind and not listening to my body or soul, I would have discounted the message even if I had heard it. *What?* I would have thought, *This is no time for the park. I need to think!* And because I wasn't following the guidance, I would have missed the lesson I got by the riverside, which led me to find the home, job, and security I was so concerned about needing.

Yes, there is always guidance from the Universe coming to us through both our souls and the entire living world. It is our choice whether or not to follow the advice.

Many of us have an "I am tough" or "I am a survivor" mentality. This bring-it-on attitude is pure critical mind. The critical monkey mind can't allow us to surrender to flow. Its entire existence is one of "I can make it happen." Choosing to rely only on yourself exclusively is a tough row to hoe. Can it be done? Yes. However, there is always a price to pay.

My dad was a self-made man in every sense of the word. His childhood was difficult. At ten years of age, he was up at 4:30 am to feed the cows and clean the barn before school. After school, he worked in a shoe store until 10:00 at night.

Before starting college, he became a marine and did very well. Then he received a degree and ended up going into the stock market. By the time he retired, he was vice president of a large brokerage firm branch in our home state.

I loved my dad! He taught me many good habits that have lasted to this day. However, his whole life revolved around work. He was always stressed. I think that is why he developed a twitch in his left eye. He simply never seemed able to slow down, like he felt he had to make things happen. He died from early-onset Lou Gehrig's disease.

To this day, I feel that if my dad had not been so stressed and had trusted that something greater was at work in his life, he would have found that he could still attain his goals while also enjoying the journey and his relationships. Even though I loved my dad and learned from him, we weren't very close until his later years, right before he became sick. He simply was too busy making things happen every minute of his life.

Here is a big truth. The Universe has you always in its sights. Divine awareness is present everywhere! Most important is that this big, beautiful Universe we are all part of, has bigger plans for us. Bigger than we could ever—not in a million years—imagine for ourselves.

We can only create that which we can imagine. Our vision for ourselves and our lives is limited, and so, what we can "make happen" is limited. The miracle is that if we surrender, believe, and allow the flow of life to happen, just like the river does, the Universe will take us to a better destination than we can imagine, one where we can end up doing so much more and helping so many more people.

So, the question always comes down to this: Do we want to keep playing it small and always be in control? Or are we brave enough to let go of the reins and trust that the Universe has our backs? Can we surrender and flow like water, which always knows where it is going, however, allows itself to trust that there are many ways to get there?

Flowing water allows itself to be guided by Mother Earth around her rocks and terrain. There is no drama or fear or defiance.

I must admit that when a mentor of mine presented me with this concept of surrender and flow, I honestly did not feel I could open up and trust enough to do it. I was my dad's daughter—I made things happen. I was a mover and shaker, and I had never heard the words, "No, it can't happen."

Like me back then, you may be thinking, *What do you mean, "Surrender and allow life to unfold"? What are you smoking?*

However, when this concept was presented to me, I also remembered how hard it was for my dad. He had missed so much of the goodness of life. Maybe there was another way. Perhaps it was time for me to explore what this was. Maybe I needed to learn to flow like water.

I must admit that surrendering seemed impossible for me at first. Just allowing life to flow sounded worse to my ears than listening to fingernails scratching a blackboard. However, I was intrigued by the concept and vowed to try different methods until I achieved a feeling of surrendered freeness. If going right into surrender was not possible for me, then I would go about it another way.

I decided to build my faith in the Divine and myself. I started to read, listen, and learn all the different ways people believed in the Beloved and the Universe. I read the words of great spiritual masters and became interested in the principles of Taoism as a way to begin to live my life in surrender to the movements of nature and the Universe. Increasingly, I began to understand that to find fulfillment and happiness I had to trust my soul and the Universe.

I began to talk to my soul more. "Are you there, Soul?" I would ask.

"Yes, I am here," was always the reply.

I discussed everything with my soul. Every idea or concept I was processing. We had long dialogues that allowed me to be open to what I heard my soul say to explicitly believe my soul's words every time I heard them.

Sometimes we edit what we hear from our souls. And an even more interesting phenomenon is that sometimes the critical mind begins to sound more like the soul. We must remember that the critical mind is part of us. And because of this, it is just as smart as us and can fool us. The only problem is that the critical mind always reveals itself because it can do only three things, attack, defend, or judge, whereas the soul is exclusively loving.

That's a great test if you are feeling doubtful about the advice you're receiving. Just ask: *Is this loving advice? Will this advice lead to a loving outcome?*

Often, dialoguing with my soul enlightened me by furthering my understanding of complex concepts and philosophies. One time, I asked my soul, "How many lives have I lived?" To my surprise, the number eight flashed in my head. My soul even began to show me images from one of those lives in bits and pieces. I saw the Baltic Sea and a cabin up on a hill with the village below. The cabin felt warm, and it was filled with herbs and jars of things. It turns out that I was a healer in that lifetime.

Whether you believe in reincarnation or not is none of my business. My point is that the soul is connected to the Universe and can reveal many truths and profound insights. Once we open to receiving the messages without judgment or defense—without the critical mind—then all sorts of information will be available to you.

Complete and Total Surrender

Even after I began conversing with my soul regularly and felt my soul with me all the time, I still had a lot to learn about surrendering completely to living by its guidance. I still had a bit of an I-can-do-it-myself attitude. But that changed once I got taught another powerful lesson about flow.

It was during the last stage of my divorce. All that was left to be determined was the support plan for our children, and we had one significant disagreement. I thought it was an important issue, but my ex did not. It was such a bone of contention that we'd gone to court many times with appeals of various judgments. Now our case was in front of the Supreme Court of our state for the second time. We had been battling for five and a half years, too long, and I was tired.

An email showed up in my inbox from a particular mentor with a link to a video in which he was saying, as he pointed his finger out from the screen, "You need to come to see me!" I had never seen this person before; however, I liked his way of making decisions, and my soul kept saying, "He has something you need to learn." So, I pointed back at the video and replied, "Yes, I do!"

So off I went to meet this gentleman and future mentor whom I knew deep in my soul could help me, although I didn't know in what way. I traveled up to Canada for his one-week event, and even though I did not know him, it was the best decision I had ever made. As I listened to him speak, my soul kept urging me, "Talk to him." Well, that proved not to be easy since this was my very first time at this event, but I was very persistent and finally found the person who managed his calendar and could set up a time for me to meet this insightful man.

This was the first time we were meeting one on one. I had wanted to sound put-together, calm, and in control when I met him. Finally, I was sitting with him, and he asked how he could help me. And the flood gates broke—everything gushed out in a weird, contorted way. Control be damned. Somehow this man heard what he needed to hear.

He paused once the flood ended and then said, "Let it all go!"

What? Did I hear him correctly? Let it go? Let what *go? The divorce? The support for my kids?* "Are you speaking ethereally?" I asked him.

"No," he assured me. "Let go of it all. You can support your kids. You don't need him."

I stared at him as my mind slowly caught up with this new idea. *Was this possible?*

As I got used to the possibility, I felt my body getting lighter. Something burdensome and heavy was leaving my energy field. I began to giggle as I thanked this new mentor of mine. Looking back on it now, he really must have thought I was crazy.

I went straight to a quiet place and called my lawyer. I heard his voicemail, and I left him a clear instruction, "Stop everything! I want to end this now." Oh, the freedom I felt! The incredibleness and lightness of being! I was free, truly free!

That was until my lawyer called me back and said it was too late. The case was before the court already.

Thus, I was about to learn how to keep my inner freedom while going through a legal process. I was about to learn how to surrender fully.

Because I was determined to keep my sense of freedom and lightness during the period of waiting for the decision to come back from the court, I decided to do a ceremony. I went out into my back yard and built a fire in the fire pit. It was a beautiful night with a full moon. I had written out what I wanted to say to the Universe, which I read out loud. "Universe, I cannot carry this load anymore. It is way too heavy for me. I must ask you to carry it. Do what you will with it. I ask only that the results be for the best of everyone involved. Thank you with my whole heart." Then, I burned the letter to send its energy up to the Universe and went to bed.

From that moment on, I put the whole affair out of my mind. I went about helping my children heal and writing a book. Every time the idea of the verdict came into my head, I would deliberately think, *For the betterment of all.*

The matter was out of my hands. It was time for my life to flow wherever it was supposed to flow. I had the faith that the Universe knew better than I how to resolve the situation.

When the decision arrived from the Supreme Court, I had lost the case. Particular issues I had long considered important would not be factored into the amount of the child support that the judge would award to my children. I could have been disappointed or upset, but I was neither. All I could think was that the Universe had decided that this outcome was what was best for all parties involved, including my children. I went on with my life feeling in flow and watching everything come together effortlessly for myself and my family.

As I was driving in a new city, going to an event for one of my children, I received a call from my ex-father-in-law telling me that he understood what I was fighting for and that I was not to worry. The needs of my children would be fully funded. This outcome was more than I ever hoped would happen. Beloved God and the Universe had done what was best for all. Having me wait for the court's decision gave me time for forgiveness and for everyone to think through what was best for the children.

Upon reflection, the process of surrendering my will ensured that I would harbor no ill-feeling, that I would stop trying to make something happen, and that I would have no residual anger when things did not go my way. I treated everyone involved, even my ex and his family, with kindness from that day forward. The victory for my ex allowed he and his family to open to healing and seeing what was needed for the children from their hearts. And the children would receive what had once been such a struggle to gain.

Water does not keep going back to the rock that once blocked it. It moves around it and then flows forward, creating life wherever it travels.

SKILLS FOR YOUR JOURNEY

It is time to open to both your soul and the Beloved as it is reflected in the physical world. Awareness and trust are the two critical skills to tune in to at the beginning of spiritual awakening. Awareness begins with trusting your intuition, and the messages you hear from your soul, and the images your soul shows you. This information is vital for your well-being and growth. Please always remember that the activities of the soul are loving, creating, and expanding. Everything it presents to you will be of goodness.

- **Start to notice and listen for the sound of goodness inside you speaking to you.** What does the voice of inner divinity want for you? Intuitive answers are always direct. This you have seen with my journey. When worry affects us, not many of us think of going to a park or river. But it was the river that allowed me to gain the answers. We choose instead to worry and listen more to the ego. Be the one to listen to the urge of the soul. Be like the water that goes around the challenge. Your soul can help you to choose a smoother path, a path of flow, and the results will be so much better than those you could generate on your own.

How does spirit show itself to you? Does a part of nature keep appearing in your life? Do you keep seeing a particular animal or plant? What can you learn from it? Do you have an urge to be by water or to sit under a tree or to take a hike?

Maybe you are facing an obstacle in your journey? Where are you being urged to go and ease your thoughts? Is it a river like it was for me? Maybe it is the strength and steadiness of a tree you are longing to sit under and unload your worries. The urge is what takes you to where you need to be to learn the lesson and gain what you need to proceed on your journey with more ease and flow.

Many times, when I have a question in my mind, or I am processing a situation, a friend or family will uncharacter-is-ti-cally and without knowing, say the most meaningful and insightful words. Pay attention and accept it, learn from it, and always say, "Thank you!

- **Trust.** Trust is the complete surrender to the knowledge of how the Divine has your back. As you take steps necessary to achieve whatever it is you want to accomplish in your life, trust. Have faith that you are, indeed, being divinely led.

For example, as I write this book, I have total faith that it will help the thousands of people who need and want it. Believing this gives me the energy I need to move forward. I trust that God/the Universe is providing me with exceptional insights and the skills necessary so that the book will be the best it can be. I do not worry or allow doubt to present me with problems to solve. Instead, I know in my heart that it will serve those who want and need it.

- **Align with your soul purpose.** What types of worry consume your thinking? Is it the thought of making money? Gaining status? Finding a soulmate? Before you ask for help and surrender those goals to the Universe, it is beneficial to determine the underlying reasons why you want these things. The answer will help you align your actions with your soul's purpose.

  For example, one of my personal goals is to earn a lot of money. I want to make lots of money because with it I can help charitable organizations and help more people. With money, I can provide for my family. With money, I can travel to different foreign countries and learn about their cultures. Those reasons give me the energy I need to take massive action in realizing my goals.

  Once you have identified the bigger reasons to want what you want—your soul's desires—then surrender your will to the will of the Universe and have total faith and trust that you will be guided as you take the steps. All will be created in the very best way possible.

Chapter 11

The Sweetness of the Sweet Spot

A life without judgment, criticism, or fear is a life of pure joy.

Magic has been coming back into my life over several years—and I always find myself going deeper. A beautiful aspect of spiritual growth is that whenever I consciously live through my soul, a veil lifts and I can see Spirit everywhere. It also is so much fun, and truly amazing, to see the love, strength, goodness, and true essence of someone's soul when I am speaking with them. More and more, I find myself talking with my soul throughout the day, and I am creating at an insane rate. It is as if my soul has been waiting for me to open up and listen to it. My kids love my openness because I am so much more available to play games or to help them with their projects and homework, and we are creating stories together. I have so much more energy than I used to; however, at certain moments, time seems to stand still.

The best part is that I feel whole in myself. Complete. I am content with who I am and the woman I am becoming. My sense of wholeness gives me a core of calmness and strength that I can draw upon when I need them. I feel confident in my abilities and ideas.

Most of all, however, I benefit from knowing I am not alone, but part of a greater energy and connected to everything in the Universe.

These days, I laugh fuller and more often. Vulnerability and authenticity are my normal modes of being and expression. Why would I want to be or communicate any other way? Or an even better question: What do I have to hide?

Life has certainly taken a turn for the better. In general, I feel as if I have made it—that I am living the magic with occasional exceptions. Sometimes the Universe has plans for me that are different from mine. Like it did the time I was invited to speak in California.

At the start of the trip, I decided to spend a free day at the Chopra Center in Carlsbad. I was eager to relax with a massage and then do a group meditation session, followed by strolling around the peaceful grounds and exploring the library. I certainly didn't expect to be pushed forward with a major insight that day, triggered by something the meditation leader said.

During the meditation, our leader spoke about the *sweet spot* in meditation and I felt that incredible peace and timelessness I've come to love.

After the meditation, he said something that really got me thinking: He said that we could live in that sweet spot if we chose.

What? I wondered. *Wouldn't that mean we would be in a weird state? I mean, would we still have the joy and the fun of life or would everything just be peaceful and timeless?* These and many other questions filled my head. I decided to stay and talk with the instructor to learn more about this possibility and what it might require of me.

He was reassuring, telling me that, no, I would not be in a timeless zombie state with no emotions or fun. *Whew!* That was a relief. He added, "It is the state of the soul, like looking at the world through the eyes of a child." He then asked me to take a moment to observe who was looking out of my eyes. I had heard this said before but never tried it until then.

What was it like? Well, once you become conscious of looking out of your eyes, you realize there is something inside you doing the looking. That's your soul.

Everything for me turns more alive and vivid when I view things through the eyes of my soul. For the soul, there is no labeling, no judgment—just seeing.

Now, here is what got me hooked on learning more about living in the sweet spot. The only thing that interrupts this view—seeing through the eyes of the soul—is the critical mind. If we judge or add labels, the critical mind takes over.

For instance, when I smell coffee in the morning, first I smell that familiar warm, delicious smell. Next my critical mind comes in and calls it *coffee.* Once it is labeled, it becomes coffee with all the descriptions and expectations of what I believe coffee to be.

I remember when I was just starting to get into gardening. I loved the plants, but I didn't know many of their names. It was their colors and textures that drew me in. I would begin to put a landscape together like an artist. Going to the plant nursery was a fun adventure. Once I had learned the names of the plants, somehow gardening lost some of its magic. I found that instead of hunting for the perfect color or texture, I would make a list of what I wanted, calling the plants by name, and having expectations of them. And that was that! The wonder and mystery were done. Now it was a description and expectation.

The meditation instructor mentioned how we also judge other people by putting expectations from our critical mind on them. And when an expectation fails or a person does something we don't expect, we become upset or surprised or pleased.

This same concept really applies to every situation in our lives. The truth is that everything just is. We are the ones who feel the impulse to define things and predict behavior.

What if we allowed ourselves not to define everything? To let the world around us do what it was going to do?

The teacher clarified the experiment we could try in our lives by suggesting that when we allow ourselves to remain in the sweet spot, we might never have the feeling of failure again because we do not have any expectations.

This was interesting. I understood what he was saying, however I had to ask, "How do we unlearn everything in our cognitive minds? How do we not put things in a category of expectation?"

His answer was, "Just let it be."

This seemed crazy—however, it intrigued me greatly! I decided to experiment with this concept for the rest of the day. I walked outside and immediately opened myself to see the vibrancy of the contrast between the green of the trees and grass and the very blue sky. Instead of allowing my mind to go into its cognitive library, furthering my description of grass and trees or even drawing forth rational explanations, like, *Why the sky is so blue today is because . . .*

Stop! I thought. *Allow it to be what it is right now in this moment. Allow yourself to feel the joy of vibrance and the feeling of vastness of the cloudless sky.*

Oh my, this felt awesome. I felt alive! I practiced living in the sweet spot at intervals for the rest of the trip, and then, when my trip was over, I continued playing around with being in the sweet spot back at home. As I allowed myself to see through the eyes of my soul, everything around me came alive. Because I wasn't busy labeling, I saw more.

I began to pet my cat, I felt the softness of the way she moved in response to the petting, the looks she gave—I saw her. When I spoke to someone, I found myself looking deeply into their eyes. I saw them for their real self, which in turn caused me to open to love. I saw the beauty and the unsureness, sometimes strength, sometimes sorrow. How could I not love the trueness and the vulnerability of them?

I began to love this way of being. I felt so free from critical mind and judgment. This made me think. *How could a person have this feeling for all of life? What would it take? How would I begin?* I decided to do another experiment.

The next morning, while in meditation, I surrendered to the feeling of spaciousness and timelessness, of nothing and everything. I felt so much happiness and love being in this space. There was a sensation of total acceptance—like being in the presence of the Beloved. I absorbed this feeling, keeping the space open inside me when I finished my meditation. I stayed in this feeling of acceptance of everything. Just being. As I took my son to school that morning, I noticed his hair needed to be brushed. Instead of judging him and telling him to brush his hair, I asked, "Do you feel you should brush your hair?" He looked at me, smiled, nodded, and took out a brush and started brushing. Stuff did not bother me. All the little things that usually would get on my nerves did not matter.

After several days passed, I noticed that I was able to stay in this state of being, which some call a Christ-like state for longer durations. I found myself beginning to think from a higher state of being or from my soul. If a situation appeared that needed attention, because I didn't enter into the drama of the moment. I could see all sorts of different advantage points with ease and decide how to solve the problem faster. There didn't seem to be a right way or a wrong way—it was more about which way would serve everyone the best.

As we previously discussed, to conclude my divorce I learned how to let go of one situation. That experience made a huge impact in my life. Now I was beginning, in a way, to let go of everything. To let it just be. With this shift, I felt a rush of freedom, and as if I could at last begin to create.

At first my critical mind fought me like crazy. How could I not be upset when my dogs broke through the fence and roamed the countryside? How could I stay in this acceptance of everything when the world was in such chaos—with people starving and policies I thought were wrong being passed by lawmakers? How could I have such peace?

My critical monkey mind then climaxed with some guilt, "Why aren't you upset? Do something? This is not a natural way to be? You're a hot-tempered Italian, for heaven sake—get upset!"

Yes, my critical mind was pulling out all the stops. However, I did not give in to it. This time I was determined that my ego was not going to win. I was using my gift of willpower to teach my whole self to "just be."

Now, I do want to insist that the intent of staying in the sweet spot is not an excuse to run around in denial of everything in the world. It doesn't require us to suddenly go live in cave and ignore the world just to have peace. This is different from denial!

From my perspective, I was allowing my soul to be an active participant in my life—I was, more and more, living from the highest part of me and totally connected to Divine. It wasn't that I didn't care about things. Instead, it was that I now understood that force is not necessary. And even more—there actually is nothing to understand. Everything simply is.

This recognition gives me the option of accepting facts and deciding how to respond to them without added drama. Wow!

For the first three days of my new commitment, I had to consciously keep myself in my sweet spot. From that point on, it was natural. If I felt my stomach stirring when something was presented to me, I would ask myself, *Why am I feeling this disturbance?* The answer really surprised me the first time I asked the question, *Because you are not controlling it.*

I have never been a control freak; however, this reply from my soul revealed to me that I had wanted to have control over things in my life even when I told myself I was letting go or surrendering. So, was I now a walking zombie? Completely in another world of bliss? No! But I felt truly alive, and it felt great. Every part of me hummed with life. It was as if the loving light was finally allowed to come through me, become me, and shine from me.

I began dealing with everything through love. Every decision I made was for the best of everyone involved. This love allowed me to see deeper into the heart of any matter. There was no or very little critical mind trying to be righteous or feeling indignant. Instead, I was able to quickly get to the heart of the problem and bring love into the situation.

A perfect example of how this works is what happened when my son told me that he didn't want to go to school anymore. Remember my story of how I opened to my soul and it responded with guidance for me to listen to him and look in his eyes?

Well, I do not need to ask my soul for special guidance anymore because I am one with my soul and living in the sweet spot. I have allowed myself to fully become my higher, true self. And really, it wasn't hard to do once it was explained to me. You can do it just like I did! The only thing I removed in order to accomplish this was my critical mind.

I often wonder if a critical monkey mind is part of a design to help us forget the higher self—the soul—so we can experience things we otherwise would not be able to experience. Without the critical mind, we would already understand because we are spirit.

Maybe, we need to understand feelings of helplessness or self-righteousness or even depression. There may be a whole bigger picture at work. This planet is our souls' world to experiment with and experience. Maybe our critical minds are part of the experience?

What I have found to be the hardest aspect of my personality to let go of is an automatic response of wanting to put others at ease. At a point when someone I am speaking with has reached a decision or I have something to say that I think they don't want to hear, I will retract from what I perceive as force and instead smile and let them off the hook by saying something funny or changing the subject another way. It is as if I do not want them to have to deal with a problem. Or maybe it is self-protective—I just don't want to get into a topic that deeply.

This behavior is automatic, so it has been more difficult for me to catch as I allow myself to embody my soul more consistently. I think this reaction stemmed from always being the Little Diplomat, as my dad used to call me. As a child, I was a cute peacemaker.

That cute peacemaker grew into a peacemaker on steroids, and for most of my life was keeping me from allowing others to get too deep with me. It is fascinating to me how the critical mind can take a simple character trait and use it in a way that holds us back or causes us problems as we try to move forward. The critical monkey mind's antics seem antithetical to our progress as souls. What once kept us safe or defined us now grips us with everything it has got.

To this day, I am still working on integrating this peacemaker with my soul purpose. It is much easier now that I can see clearly that it isn't my job to stop others from evolving their souls by wrestling with their issues on their own. When I am invited to mentor people or teach a group of individuals how to speak to their souls, I can be there to listen or to prompt them with a question to look at their situation in a different way. Maybe this is why my clients call me the Soul Nurturer—because I offer suggestions that bring them more ease in their process of growth.

The integrated peacemaker has skills that will be very useful in my pursuit of this purpose. My soulful purpose is to bring people to the light as I do with some people who pass on in their journey. Even though every part of my being, including my critical mind, wanted this purpose, there were still beliefs and thoughts in my critical mind that would stop my dream. One of these was my peacemaker. Once I came to the realization that there was a good side to the peacemaker, my critical mind no longer could use it to sabotage me. In fact, my mind consciously brings it forward in a better way to help me be more effective with my beautiful clients.

Letting go of the critical mind has created a different experience in how I help my clients. I truly laugh so much easier and find joy in every day of living. Wherever I am, I am at ease. So, I am open and present when I am helping them as well. I allow myself to be guided by my soul for how to be with them instead of attempting to control them. When I help others, I present options, ideas, and concepts I know are valuable and have worked for others in similar situations. I encourage their efforts and most of all give them loving guidance. I do not tell them, "This is how it must be."

There is no one way, no pill to take that awakens you to your soul—you do it how you do it, and it works. Each person knows what they need, so helping them open their awareness or giving them a tool to get started, and then guidance, is the extent of what I do.

Things that used to bother me just do not bother me anymore. It is not that I let anyone take advantage of me or hurt me. I still take care of what needs to be done. But the drama and the craziness that used to be involved are gone. Because I come from a place of love, solutions present themselves in an easier way for the benefit of all.

Nothing has to be difficult anymore.

I love living from my soul. I love how it has opened my whole life to love. I love feeling the vibrancy of life and perceiving beauty in others. I wish for all people to see the beauty that rests inside them as I do.

SKILLS FOR YOUR JOURNEY

Now it is your turn to become one with your soul. Remember to take your time. Evolution comes when we are ready for it. This whole chapter is an exercise for you to try, so you may want to read it again before doing the exercises below, or maybe you're ready to try them right now. Either way, the important thing is to be patient with yourself. Allow instead of making it happen.

- **To understand what the sweet spot feels like, do a short meditation and open to the space between the in and out breath.** Then, allow yourself to go deeper, becoming more relaxed while staying in the vast spaciousness of the sweet spot you drop into. Soon you will be able to remain in that amazing state of being for up to twenty minutes. You are on your way.

  While you are awake, try to stay in that spot. Remember how I went outside and saw the trees and the blue sky? I did not label or judge the awesome deep blue of the sky and the vivid green foliage standing out against it. Allow yourself to maintain a peaceful sense of aliveness for as long as you can. Each time you reach the sweet spot you will be able to keep it longer.

  What an incredible feeling it is—so freeing.

- **Play the game I played when I petted my cat.** Let's call it the No Label Game. Create some time in your day just to observe the world without analyzing its qualities. Don't try to define anything other than the immediate. With my cat, I allowed myself to feel the softness of her fur, to look into her eyes without judging, summarizing, or labeling.

  You do the same. Just allow everything to be as it is without interpretation. What this opens you to is the experience, and the result is feeling something new that brings you alive inside. When you speak to people, be engrossed with what they are saying. If you don't try to comment or summarize what they are saying, you will find that a beautiful story develops, and you will see them for who they are in that moment.

Life comes alive!

Chapter 12
True Manifesting with Soul

Manifesting a life without worry, strife, or feelings of lack is what every person on Earth wants. Is it possible? Anything is possible once we understand!

I have done it! I am living through my soul. There is this incredible feeling of peace and love. Meditation comes so easy and life is full of fun because I enjoy with love my interaction with friends, colleagues, and my family. The best part is that I find people respond to the love they feel from me. This creates a wonderful trust between us and deeper friendships.

But it wasn't always this way. Until recently, when I began to think about my business, my stomach would get a funny feeling—not of worry, but of slight agitation—and doubt would enter my mind. This did not feel good. I then would wonder, *Alright, why am I having this sudden disconnect? Is there a way to have something I desire and still be living as my soul?*

Whenever this would happen, I tried using affirmations. Some of them helped me reconnect with my soul. To be honest, however, when I spoke affirmations, I sometimes felt that I was just pushing down the doubt. It wasn't really leaving me.

There had to be a way to let the doubt totally leave my mind and body. I wanted no obstacles between me and my soul and the Universe.

This type of question initiated a new inner journey for me. Over many years, I have attended lectures, listened to audios, and watched videos of different spiritual teachers talking about the concepts of desire and attachment. According to them, when the mind loves an idea or object, it can become attached to it. An attachment causes us to become worried or angry if we are threatened with losing the object of our desire. Also, if we have trouble attaining something we desire.

Here's a simple example. Let's say I am accustomed to having a latte every morning. I am attached to the ritual of getting one from the same coffee shop each day. I believe it "wakes me up" and "gets me ready for a productive day." One morning, the line was too long when I arrived, and I did not have time to wait to get my latte. I may become angry or upset. I may worry about being sleepy.

Of course, this is a super simple example. However, are the feelings of worry and anxiety the same or even more intense when we are attached to a particular outcome, such as reaching our goals, and believe they are important?

Here's another example. Say I want to make a million dollars this year in my company. I have the plan, the product, and the people to make this happen. I plan each step my company will take and believe I can predict the outcome. I am attached to reaching that million. Even more to the point, I equate my happiness and success with reaching my financial goal. I may be planning the trips I will take and the stuff I will buy to reward myself.

Why spiritual gurus say this kind of attachment is a problem does not depend on the outcome—whether it is a cup of coffee or a cool million. The problem is the attachment; and the reasons are twofold. An obvious problem occurs when a plan does not get realized. If I don't receive the result I thought would happen, then worry and anger enter my mind and body. *Why didn't my plan work?* I wonder. I begin to scrutinize everything in my plan. Every step of my activity after that becomes tedious and hard, filled with expectation and doubt.

The other problem with an attachment (let's say to my million-dollar goal) is that the object of the attachment becomes my ideal source of happiness. Just like with the latte, I believe that I cannot be happy unless I attain my goal in the way I expect to attain it.

If I am unsuccessful in attaining my desired outcome, I feel unhappy and think of myself as a failure.

Should I not have desire? Should I just let everything in my life unfold without putting any skin in the game? Should I retire to a hidden place on a mountainside, far away from the demands and expectations of the world?

There are many spiritual teachers who proclaim that they are free and happy because they have no attachments or desires. But can we really experience no desire? Isn't wanting not to have desire a desire too? Interesting paradox, isn't it?

I have many friends who live very simply, just loving the world around them, without desire or setting any goals. Are they happier without experiencing a desire to achieve anything? Not really. Many seem to worry and anguish anyhow.

To have a desire deep inside you to create something is natural and good. This urge comes from your soul.

I do not agree with the gurus that all desire is bad. I think soulful desire is good and gives us purpose. I do feel, however, that when we put demands on how and when the objects of our desire will arrive we are forming an attachment to an outcome. There is nothing wrong in the desire itself, only in how we treat the desire. Is it possible to have the desire and take the steps to enjoy and build it—to just trust, enjoy, and be with the desire without all the expectation, goal setting, and wanting of a certain outcome? Yes! It is very possible. Granted it is not what our western society prides itself on however, it is really what our soul is here to do. It is living the creating of experiences and life.

As I am writing this book, I am enjoying the process of learning more about hearing my soul. I am sitting outside on a beautiful Saturday morning, writing. I am not thinking, *This book will make millions.* In fact, I am not putting any sort of expectation on this project. Instead, I am just enjoying sharing my journey with anyone who also wants that journey.

And I must say, this approach to writing a book is incredibly fun and freeing. It opens me to loving my desire to be useful to all the people who want to learn and grow. I want to share more and make sure my writing is perfectly clear. I want to bring my best to that desire.

What about when you are presented with an opportunity that tickles your desire but is not yet fully in your heart? This could be a desire for a job promotion, a desire to veer into a new area in your business or life, or a desire to make a change in your lifestyle. The opportunity looks good and would be beneficial for your growth. Under these conditions, how can you check with your heart, see if the opportunity fits your desire, and let go of the worry of making it happen?

Here's an example of an opportunity becoming a soulful desire that occurred back in my unconsciously competent days when I was working at a university teaching voice, opera, and music history.

Several weeks into the fall semester, the director of the music department called me into his office and asked me to start a women's choir at the university. My subconscious mind had a field day. I thought, *I don't have a degree in conducting. The faculty will make mincemeat out of me. I have no business conducting for a university, as I am not skilled enough.*

The director was not interested in my limitations. He had recently heard me direct a church choir and was impressed. In his mind, I was now the director of the new women's choir.

Posed with this opportunity, despite my subconscious concerns, I figured that I could either continue to worry that I wasn't qualified or I could do my best to give the young women who joined the choir the best opportunity to learn something incredible and bring pride to our music department. I went home, made a cup of tea, and sat myself down underneath a big tree in my backyard.

This tree was my "thinking tree." It had a thick trunk and the energy of strength and possibility. I loved sitting in the shade beneath its leafy branches and immersing myself in its strength. Whenever I would relax under this particular tree, I always found my creative mind opening to the world of ideas, a world that Neville Goddard calls the "formless substance" in his book *The Power of Awareness.*[5]

On this particular occasion, I began to open the door to my creative spirit by asking myself a starter question: *Why do I love music so much?*

An answer came: *Because the progressive harmonies, rhythm, and combinations of instruments along with voices paint pictures in my mind. They build a story!*

I continued my internal dialogue from there. *Okay, so why would the women want to sing in the choir?*

Answer: *Because I am a singer. I know how to use the voice to paint colors and textures to make a "painting" come alive. These women will learn not only to sing together, but also to create sounds they never thought possible. They will be able to work the sound of the vowels and consonants and the volume of their voices and learn to move as one in a miraculous way.*

Question: *And why will people come to hear our choir?*

Answer: *Because they cannot get this type of experience anywhere else.*

My mind was filled with the future sounds of this amazing choir. I could hear its magnificent, unified harmony surrounding me. This was going to be an amazing experience. I thanked my tree with a big hug and went inside to pick out music to begin.

This choir started with ten women. By the second semester, there were twenty-five in the choir. Each semester the ranks of the choir grew. The rehearsals were experimental in a way that created incredible chances for each student to discover her ability and the possibilities of her voice. The singers loved the sound and feeling as their voices moved as one, especially on a vocal slide. They almost cried the first time they learned to make the free-floating sound of a high A sung pianissimo. One choir member said she felt the effortless floating feeling of the sound was like an "intense feather."

The whole time I conducted I was having fun. I really didn't think beyond making each rehearsal a magical world of sound. Where this choir was going did not matter to me as I was fully immersed in the journey of creating.

After one of our performances, a prominent conductor from our area came up to me and asked, "Do you have a doctorate yet?" I looked her straight in the eye and replied that I did not. She then invited me to meet her in the parking lot of the school the next morning. She said she wanted me to come with her to meet someone.

Intrigued, I met her the next morning and we drove down to another university that was her alma mater. There, the conductor marched me up the stairs of the music department and introduced me to its director. Before I knew it, I was registered in the school. I had been accepted into a doctoral program for conductors with a full assistantship, which meant I would be working as the conductor for two of the choirs at the university and grading papers for the music history undergrad courses.

Why do I tell this story? Because it helps me to remember how life unfolds in unbelievable ways when we let go of the result.

Back to our discussion of desire and creativity. Things happened effortlessly for me whenever I followed my desire to create without attachment but only because I was having fun building and being present and alive in every glorious moment of my life. I got the opportunity to study conducting even though I did not focus on "being discovered" or "making lots of money." In fact, I didn't even think about being the top choir at the school or going down in history as an innovator. I only wanted to create an experience for myself and for these young women. I wanted them to feel good about themselves and their abilities and show them what they could create together.

Every moment of the choir experience was precious and fun. Conducting the choir was an experiment and I was not attached to any particular outcome. Being open gave me freedom to really focus on each moment in our rehearsals and be creative. Because there was no real attachment to the outcome, there was no worry or anxiety.

If no one had showed up for the choir on the first day of rehearsal, I would have been fine. That would have meant it simply was not time for the choir. No big deal—I was not attached.

The ancient Chinese text *Tao Te Ching*, which I so greatly admire, is all about how we can enjoy the journey of life, which then turns into connection to Divine Source.[4] One stanza reads: "Do that which consists in taking no action and order will prevail." After studying this passage, I believe it means that if we stop forcing ourselves to meet a goal or desire and instead become comfortable doing less, albeit still creating and having fun, we stop breaking the true connection to Divine Source. This leaves room for its creation to work through us.

As I look back at those days, I never felt an attachment to a particular goal. I loved to sing and to help others to awaken a similar love. This ability not to feel attached to specific outcomes is the key to living without the vices of guilt, worry, anger, shame, and pressure.

Without these destructive emotions, we are left with happiness, lightness, love, and freedom of creativity.

None of us has to live on a mountain in solitude or allow life to just be, unless this is what is desired and we have the financial freedom to do so. We can have fun creating and experiencing. This is what our soul craves. It is why we are here on this earth. It is only when we let the ego or critical mind pollute our thoughts with its demands to pursue that we become disconnected from our true essence and the Divine.

Well, let me put your ego mind to rest. You can have success and still consider yourself a soulful person. The acclaimed twentieth-century motivator Earl Nightingale had a definition of success that is beautiful. "Success is the progressive realization of a worthy ideal."[6] Absolutely perfect! I wholeheartedly agree. This is a description of the philosophical concept of *wu wei,* a Taoist term that means "effortless action."

As we create, have fun, and move forward in learning, growing, and becoming everything that we become, we are successful. Why? Because creating, learning, growing, and becoming are the activities that teach us the lessons our souls need to evolve. The soul does not devolve due to the attainment of different goals. It grows in the journey to reach every goal. That journey gives meaning to our life.

I have decided to apply this way of living—the *Wu Wei* approach—to the here and now. As I sit in my comfy chair on a Sunday evening, a time I formerly would reserve for planning my accomplishments and goals for the week ahead, I instead choose to write down what I want to create and try to define what will help the people I serve the very best. In this writing, I also include details about how I personally want to grow and what I want to learn more about.

No more do I feel agitation in my stomach or the doubt entering my mind when I think about my business. I no longer do affirmations. Instead I am open to living each day open to experience life to its fullest and have the fun of creating my hearts' desire whatever that may be.

And here is the exciting part! In the last two months, as I was busy creating using the wu wei approach, my business took an amazing turn. The new marketing team I hired is totally in sync with my way of living and has turned their creativity into an incredible creative force. New ideas and possibilities are appearing right before my eyes for how to bring everything I do to more people who want to learn. Having confidence in my staff frees me to be more creative and spend time on activities such as writing *Hello, Soul!,* starting a YouTube channel for people interesting in living daily, practical spirituality, and as opportunities come to me, I am now the host of an awesome radio/podcast show - Magical Moments.

The best part of the changes I am experiencing is that I am able to live more and more with, and from connection with my soul which is allowing me to release any fear and simply create in my life. I am loving every part of this journey!

LIFE SKILLS FOR YOUR JOURNEY

Learning the skill of letting go of all attachment and still enjoying the process is wu wei. This way of creating and experiencing with the Beloved makes life a joy to live every day. Here are a couple of introspection exercises to practice as needed.

- **Look for the sources of your discomfort in your life.** Where in life does angst appear? In setting goals? Your career? Trying to achieve something in your life? Trying to meet others' demands? Whatever the source for your angst is, if tension, worry, and anxiety are present, then it is a sign of attachment. It is time to get comfortable in your sacred space, listen to wonderful calming music, and ask yourself gently, *What is it that I am attached to? What kind of outcome? Do I need to be attached to an outcome? Am I doing this activity just for the outcome?* These questions will strip away the façade of "I have to ….." and instead begin to bring you back to what really matters.

Be persistent. Don't allow excuses or other people's beliefs be your reason for allowing yourself to be attached and feel all the worry, expectation and anxiousness. This is about you and only you, and it is a great way to get down to your heart and your personal soul driven desire.

- **Imagine creation for its own sake.** Have a desire? Now it is time to create without the attachment to the outcome. What happens if the outcome is taken away? What if money didn't matter? What if fame was not real? What would happen if tomorrow you got up and just wanted to create in your work, family, or life? What if it is all just an elaborate creating game? Imagine how you would feel and what you would do.

Most of my unconsciously competent days were just like this—filled with creating and loving the process. This really is the ultimate way of living. We spend so much time trying to create to a designated end. What is wrong with just creating for the act of creation? Why do we have to put a goal on it? Once the goal has been let go then life opens new wonders. This is when I began to notice the sky and how it seems to open to the Beloved and the Universe. This is when synchronicity appeared in a major way in my life.

It is time to trust the universe. Time to let yourself know what you truly are here for and let go of what you deem any outcome should be. You will only be limited by your beliefs. The Universe and God, the Beloved, are not limited in any manner—they are infinite.

When you are ready to release your expectations and start enjoying the creative process and trusting that the very best will come, let go. Let your flow begin NOW!

To all who have joined me in reading about my soul-discovering journey—and entering into your own—congratulations! This journey is a way of making our way back to our spiritual home or source. Saying "Hello, Soul," is the secret to maintaining the well-being of our entire being, both spiritually and physically. And it is the first step in attaining permanent, ever-lasting peace, joy, and self-love.

Enjoy this beautiful spiritual space – your soul space. But please realize it is not the end. Doesn't your soul always want to grow, create, and experience? Mine does. If you haven't figured it out yet, (but I bet you already did), this whole book has been an invitation to join me in opening your connection to the Beloved and the wonders of our universe of light.

Chapter 13
Neverending Soul Evolution

*The soul replied, saying, "What binds me has been slain, and
what surrounds me has been destroyed, and my desire has
been brought to an end, and ignorance has died."²*
—Cynthia Bourgeault, *The Meaning of Mary Magdalene*

I n the chapters of this book, I spoke about the divine gift that
the Universe gave me at the early age of seven: an ability to
guide lost spirits into the light. In my innocence, I thought
everyone would rejoice with the amazing trust the Universe
had in me, a mere child. Instead, I was told that I had an evil
imagination. This began the binding of my soul.

As I came into my high school years, there was further
harsh criticism in regard to my choice of career, my independence, and my giving of my virginity to a man I loved and

thought I would marry. The constant pressure on me to conform was another binding of my soul.

Lessons in conformity are what Mary Magdalene in the
Gospel of Mary calls the "building of the ego.⁹" She was re-
ferring to the crazily critical monkey mind in our heads. The
ego wraps itself around the soul, binding it to the illusion of
only one reality (conformity). Our souls were never supposed
to live in a reality of mundane sameness.

In my early adulthood, as an unconscious competent, I was
constantly being pulled by others to live within this one reality
illusion. Every time I was pulled into the mundane, I lost more
of the magic and connection to my soul and the Divine.

My journey since then has been a journey of awareness
and awakening. The key of awareness unlocked the chains allowing my soul to break free and begin to sing. Every step of
the journey awakened a new awareness in me that enabled me
to trust the purity, simplicity, and loving guidance of my soul.
Awakening really is a gentle process, and I think that is why so
many people do not trust it.

So often, when we want freedom, we think we must slay
the critical mind, as if it is some kind of dragon. But the more
we view awakening as a fight, the more fear enters into the
transformation of our consciousness creating difficulties for
the journey.

As my awareness grew, I learned that the critical mind was
not a dragon, but a part of me; I could understand its story
and let it go.

Someone once told me that awareness is the peeling away
of each layer to our higher self or soul. I prefer to think of

awareness as the key that unlocks each chain, freeing my soul and heart more and more. I love this imagery because as each chain breaks free, I am flying higher and higher. As I shed the critical monkey mind/ego and allowed myself to accept and honor the purest form of myself, a darkness was lifted, and I became more aligned with my soul.

Once my ignorance was gone, I understood that I was a beautiful spirit full of love and light, here simply to live and experience this plain of existence. I understood with absolute clarity that my soul was my connection to the Universe and God, whom I call the Beloved because it feels as if I have fallen in love when I am in communion with it. And now I feel open to trusting the guidance and the pure love I feel every day.

I now own my power.

After many years of meditation and speaking with my soul, eventually I arrived at a feeling of owning my own power—and it was different from what I expected. I always had thought that a spiritual awakening would be more like fireworks, that if I "arrived" I would feel a surge of energy, or that there would be an I-could-climb-every-mountain kind of feeling.

These days, having gone far enough on my journey, I feel a sense of calming aliveness inside me. That's the only way I can think of to describe it. I feel a moving stream of energy creating inside of me—and I simply cannot get enough of it.

As I finish this book, I have been starting an herb garden, learning how to transform a vanity into something that looks antique, and composing a song. The many directions that my creative energy can move all at once amaze me.

The biggest chain that I unlocked and freed myself of was the chain of chasing after goals and measuring my value as a person by my achievements. I feel a lot more peace when I am creating now because I am creating from love and joy instead of from the belief that I am supposed to. Or out of worry that if I don't hurry and put pressure on myself, I will lose something—perhaps approval or status or something else. I was apprehensive about releasing the chain of my desire for achievement. I actually thought I would be bored without goals—or even worse, lost. Who would I be without constantly reaching for success and acknowledgment? Would I ever get anything done? Would I become a lazy person? I am happy to report that things still get done—and I am enjoying the doing much more.

Before, I never realized how my attachment to pursuing success prevented me from forming closer connections to people and closed me off to the sacred experience of living in the moment without an agenda. Now, having let go of this chain, I am free to be and do whatever I want without needing a reason and without having an attachment to whether or not what I am doing gets done on a certain schedule or format. Life truly has become a life of direct experience. I experience and create things without having to make them huge or have big plans.

As I live from my soul, I have a greater understanding of the reasons why I wore a chain of desire for achievement. I always felt I had to prove the validity of my choices in life to my family and demonstrate that I was being fruitful. If I didn't gain success in my chosen pursuits, then my family would let me know that they believed I could not make accurate decisions for myself. OMG! My whole life has been based on defiance of my family and proving my worthiness to live as I wanted to live.

What I now find a little funny and extremely interesting in retrospect is that whenever I did listen to my family's advice and conform to their expectations, I would be plunged into mundaneness. On their path my life would lose its magic and I would lose myself. I guess I had to take some detours to gain enough curiosity to engage fully in the journey back to my soul—to the essence of me.

As you make the same journey to find yourself and live in alignment with guidance from your soul, it will be important for you to see the history of your life from your soul's vantage point. It is important to learn this lesson because it is the highest lesson that your soul wants to teach you. This lesson is much easier to learn if you look at yourself with love. The human heart is more receptive to learning without anger or sadness, so love will help you see better and move forward with increased clarity and awareness. It will also accelerate your growth.

I have a friend who can take me back to the many lives I have lived. Yes, I am speaking about reincarnation. I had never given a thought to whether I had lived before; however, I know that we are spirit and spirit is energy. "Energy is!" (A quote from Albert Einstein.)[8] What Einstein meant is that energy cannot die or disappear. It can mutate or transform. For example, water in its drinkable state is liquid, but when subject to cold it freezes into ice, and when heated it evaporates and turns into steam. This is the same with energy: Energy is, and it has different forms!

Somewhere deep inside me, I have always known I came to earth before. I can't tell you how, but there was just this knowing that I had played the game before. So, when my friend told me she helps people go back to their past lives, I didn't even blink an eye. Actually, it caused my curious nature to awaken. Why not give it a try?

As she guided me into a very relaxed meditation. I saw different scenes from my past lives. I have lived many times. The life that piques my interest the most was one that took place during the 1800s in Italy. I was the daughter of a well-off family and a daddy's girl. I loved my dad and he thought I was very intelligent, had a mind for business, and also strong. He raised me to believe in myself and my ideas; however, when I turned eighteen and it was time for me to marry, he chose a family that would be an alliance with our business and position in the city. The man I was to marry was cold and did not value women for anything more than position. I did marry him and grew bitter and cold in that lifetime.

Why was this interesting to me? Because my lifetime in Italy ran parallel to my current life. My dad had felt the exact same way about me, and I was my daddy's girl. When I was twenty-six, he wanted me to marry—and marry "well," which to him meant marrying someone with money or status, a guy he felt would elevate my station in life. I always had felt that if I were successful in my own right, my dad would see my worth and not feel I needed to marry or "be taken care of," as he put it when we spoke of the subject.

My two lives have been similar—with one big difference. In my current life, I have corrected my path. I have chosen growth and connection rather than growing old and bitter in a loveless marriage. I left an unhappy situation instead of staying where I was told to stay, and with this choice I evolved my soul.

I share this story simply to show that we all are here to evolve our souls. This is why our experiences of creating what our heart wants us to create is so important. Our souls' lessons help us to move forward spiritually.

And almost always there is something bigger at play than we know—a more significant reason to be living.

Speaking for myself, I truly feel I am living this life to learn to free my soul.

Once we free our souls and are open to living from them/ with them fully inhabiting us, we are not confined by any chains. The soul's presence frees us from ignorance. Ignorance, as stated in the quote at the beginning of this chapter.

In saying, "And ignorance has died," Mary Magdalene meant that ignorance comes from lack of awareness. This is the ignorance of darkness. Once we open to the soul's awareness[7] and gain its perspective, once we are living from the soul, then our ignorance dies. We have taken off the weird glasses and now can see everything extremely clearly. We see everything through the eyes of love.

When it comes from the unconditional love that only the soul and the Divine Beloved provide, we are empowered.

The Next Journey

As challenges fade into lessons, relationships deepen, fun and laughter come easily, and negative emotions fade fast if they are felt, I am beginning to feel an urge.

I was in California speaking with a healer from India. We were having coffee and trading ideas. I was sharing the story of my journey of opening to my soul and he was rejoicing as I described each step. When I was done, he said, "Now it is time for you to unite with the Universal Spirit." He then went on to tell me about Buddhism's eightfold path to enlightenment. Buddhists believe the ultimate desire of every soul is to unite with spirit and that you must master eight steps before you reach enlightenment.

Uniting with spirit was the urge I was feeling. Although I am sure it would be an amazing adventure, I do not feel a need to become Buddhist or follow their path. My heart, instead, was guiding me to learn more about Mary Magdalene, starting with her gospel.

I am curious to learn how to be more open to spirit and to write about the seven levels of wrath that are described in *The Gospel of Mary*[9]. Many know these levels as "seven demons," but this is not as was told in the Bible and many have come to believe – wrath, gluttony, hate…. Instead they are the part of ourselves that keep us from a total connection with Beloved. In writing about them, I may even bring in a little information from my friends who are shamans and other spiritual teachers I know and respect.

I can feel the new journey begin in my heart. It is going to be an amazing journey. I can tell because I can feel my soul beginning to sing!

About the Author

Referred to by many as a soul curator, **Alena Chapman** works her "magic" by wisely integrating the wisdom of various religions, spiritual modalities, and scientific research to bring clarity, ease, and flow along with greater understanding to all. She's on a quest to help people everywhere heal and connect to their soul's purpose and experience abundance while on the journey. She works with clients around the world to help them learn to heal themselves so they can identify what they are really here to achieve in life, from a space of compassion, non-judgment, and love.

Alena has been a guest on ABC, CBS, PBS, iHeartRadio, Law of Attraction Radio, many conferences, interviews and events including with Les Brown and Bob Proctor and Elizabeth Gilbert. A certified counselor with Right Relations, Alena has also studied with Dr. Wayne Dyer, Bob Proctor, and countless others on top of her personal studies.

Endnotes

1. Gilbert and Sullivan, *HMS Pinafore* (reference) p. 13
2. James Allen, *As a Man Thinketh.: From Poverty to Power. The Magic is in the Stillness* (J.M.W. Group, Inc.) Be still my heart! p. 39
3. Dr. Wayne Dyer, *The Magic is in the Stillness* (reference) p. 50
4. Lao Tzu's, Tao Te Ching, *The Magic is in the Stillness; Hearing Your Soul; Flow Like Water* (Penguin Group, (USA) Inc.) p. 49, 50, 51, 52,153,189
5. Neville Goddard, *The Power of Awareness* (Merchant Books) p. 186
6. Earl Nightengale, *The Strangest Secret* (Shippensburg, PA., Sound Wisdom) Success is the progressive realization of a worthy idea p. 189
7. Cynthia Bourgeault, *The meaning of Mary Magdalene: Discovering the Woman at the Heart of Christianity* (Boston, MA.: Shambhala) Ignorance has died. p. 201
8. Albert Einstein, *The Sweetness of the Sweet Spot*, Energy Is! p. 199
9. The Gospel of Mary Building of the ego, Seven demons p. 196, 202

More Skills for
Your Spiritual Journey

$$- \Diamond -$$

ENJOYED HELLO SOUL?
Then consider leaving a review at your favorite online bookstore.

UNLOCK YOUR TRUE PASSION OF SELF
www.alenachapman.com

Here You'll Find:
Free Boundaries Quiz, Illusion and the Art of Manifestation, InevitableU, Chat's with Alena, Meditations and much more for a community of those wanting to grow on their spiritual journey. People just like You!

JOIN ME ON MY SOCIAL PAGES
YouTube/Alena Chapman
Instagram.com/Alena Chapman
TikTok.com/Alena Chapman

Catch Alena's Show 'Mystical Muse'
for the essence of your spirituality. Enjoy listening to others and their powerful spiritual journeys.
All podcast stations and YouTube

$$- \Diamond -$$

Want to Study with Alena!
alenachapman.com/contact page

All Interviews and Speaking Interests
Alenachapman.com/contact page

A free ebook edition is available with the purchase of this book.

To claim your free ebook edition:

1. Visit MorganJamesBOGO.com
2. Sign your name CLEARLY in the space
3. Complete the form and submit a photo of the entire copyright page
4. You or your friend can download the ebook to your preferred device

Print & Digital Together Forever.

Snap a photo

Free ebook

Read anywhere

Printed in the USA
CPSIA information can be obtained
at www.ICGtesting.com
JSHW022327140824
68134JS00019B/1341